SOUL-CENTERED

Soul-Centered

SPIRITUALITY FOR
PEOPLE ON THE GO

Rev. Jim Clarke, PhD

Paulist Press
New York / Mahwah, NJ

Cover image courtesy of Digital Stock
Cover design by Sharyn Banks
Book design by Lynn Else

Library of Congress Cataloging-in-Publication Data

Clarke, Jim (James J.)
    Soul-centered : spirituality for people on the go / Rev. Jim Clarke, PhD.
        pages cm
    Includes bibliographical references.
    ISBN 978-0-8091-4919-3 (pbk. : alk. paper) — ISBN 978-1-58768-483-8 (ebook)
    1. Christian life—Catholic authors. 2. Spiritual life—Catholic Church. 3. Spirituality—Catholic Church. I. Title.
    BX2350.3.C58 2015
    248.4`82—dc23

2014050068

ISBN 978-0-8091-4919-3 (paperback)
ISBN 978-1-58768-483-8 (e-book)

Published by Paulist Press
997 Macarthur Boulevard
Mahwah, New Jersey 07430

www.paulistpress.com

Printed and bound in the
United States of America

To my large and loving family, who taught me about love and laughter, acceptance of limitations, the challenges of relationships, and the overarching presence of God in the daily work of becoming a mature human person.

Contents

Acknowledgments ix

Introduction xi

Chapter 1:   Slow Down. *You're Movin' Too Fast* 1

Chapter 2:   Solitude. *Leave Me Alone* 9

Chapter 3:   Sacrifice. *Offer It Up* 15

Chapter 4:   Saints. *I Want to be in That Number* 21

Chapter 5:   Sense of Humor. *That's a Good One!* 27

Chapter 6:   Service. *How May I Help You?* 33

Chapter 7:   Sexuality. *It's Not Just about SEX!* 39

Chapter 8:   Silence. *Sh-hhhhhhhh* 47

Chapter 9:   Simplification. *Drop Your Bundle* 53

Chapter 10: Symbolic Life. *Everything Ain't What It Seems* 59

Chapter 11: Spaciousness. *Make Room: Here Comes Everything* 67

Chapter 12: Stillness. *Stop! In the Name of Love!* 73

Chapter 13: Surrender. *I Give Up!* 81

Chapter 14: Support. *We're All in This Together* 89

Chapter 15: Sustenance. *What Must I Do to Survive?* 95

Contents

Chapter 16:   Source of Income. *Paying the Bills—*
              Blood, Sweat, and Tears 103

Chapter 17:   Soulful Living. *Get Your Act Together!* 111

Chapter 18:   Signs of Holiness. *How Am I Doing?* 117

Final Thoughts: Setting Out for the Future.
              Where Do We Go from Here? 127

Works Cited 129

Acknowledgments

Any book is the work of many people, and so it is with this manuscript. I would like to acknowledge those individuals who have had a particular influence in the germination and writing of this book.

- To Joan Corfee, whose life experience and theological questions over many years have challenged me to think more expansively and adventurously about life, love, friendship, and the process of becoming fully human, fully alive. I thank her for her styling and editorial suggestions and contribution in shaping the content of this book.
- To Richard Rohr, who has formed me as a spiritual son and friend over many years of mutual collaboration. I thank him for his confidence in me and his soulful approach to the understanding of the gospel message and its proclamation.
- To Ronald Rolheiser, who has helped me to understand more clearly the theological implications of the spiritual life and what it means to live a Christian anthropology. I thank him for his insightful writing and patient persistence in sharing this message so faithfully.
- To Joan Chittister, who has demonstrated courage and compassion in the exploration of what it means to be a disciple of Christ in these challenging times. I thank her for her wisdom and clarity of insight that has encouraged me to pursue my own spiritual journey.

- To Jack Redmond, who has joined me on the journey as friend and companion and has helped me to formulate my thoughts more clearly and consistently. I thank him for his encouragement, constant affirmation, and generous spirit.
- To Robert Johnson, who has mentored me over the years in books and conversations about the vagaries of the human soul. I thank him for his tenacious love and commitment to the healing work of the human person and the soul of the world.
- To my directees, who through the sharing of their own faith stories and questions have enlivened me and expanded my perception of God's work. I thank you for your confidence in me and inviting me to journey with you.
- To Donna Crilly, my ever-patient editor, who encouraged me to put my thoughts in written form. I thank her for her helpful insights and support in moving this manuscript to completion.

Introduction

One day, Nasruddin was taking the train to his regular destination in the Punjab when the conductor approached the passengers asking for their tickets. Upon being asked for his ticket, Nasruddin began to look anxiously through his briefcase, his pants pockets, his wallet, all with no success. Finally, the conductor encouraged Nasruddin to look in the breast pocket of his coat. "That's where you normally keep it" he said. "Ah, yes, that is true," Nasruddin replied with great agitation. "But what if it is not there? I will have no other place to look!"

Have you lost your ticket on the train of life? Do you feel as if you're adrift, or caught in the extreme busyness of your life's expectations? Perhaps the Church, or your place of worship, no longer feeds your soul or has failed to keep up with the times? Perhaps you feel as if you are no longer energized, enlivened, or inspired by your faith community in these postmodern times? Or maybe you just feel disconnected from your deepest self or are seeking a more meaningful life? If any of this is true, then this book is for you!

I am writing for people who are incessantly on the go, and sense an inner restlessness or disconnectedness from their spiritual reality. This book will help you to see and understand the difference between a healthy spirituality and a toxic religious belief system. With the help of this book you will be able to create your own energizing spirituality, perhaps drawing on the different wisdom traditions of ancient religions as well as your own Christianity, if that is your faith tradition.

Spirituality is neither exotic nor elite. It is an ordinary, everyday business that doesn't require advanced study or countless hours of prayer and introspection. Rather it is a disciplined, focused attention to what is real or life-giving, demanding a lifetime of maturation, adapting, and striving for the highest values, the greatest good, and ultimate intimacy with God. Spirituality is a practice aimed at developing purity of heart, a condition in which our hearts are whole and free to love. We do this work in order to develop a stronger, more durable connection with all parts of our life. It is similar to creating a mosaic or tapestry with its many different layers or strands. The more well-placed strands that are woven together, the more durable the art piece is going to be.

Each chapter offers simple questions to stimulate your thought process in developing or integrating the different components of a vital or transformative spirituality. Specific prayer forms and spiritual practices from a variety of spiritual traditions are suggested to assist you in creating your own framework for attending to your interior life. Finally, I offer you some recommended reading if you would like to further explore a specific chapter topic. These chapters can be read quickly, in sequence or separately, depending upon your own particular interest. The book can be used for individual nourishment, adult study groups, or a group retreat.

There are numerous academic books written on the field of spirituality and spiritual theology, but very few written with the layperson in mind. I am writing from a pastoral, practical, and psychological perspective, to help you in your own spiritual development. As a spiritual director, with over thirty years of training and experience, as well as many years as a professor of spiritual theology, I am writing to "believers in exile" as well as those who sense that their spiritual lives could be richer.

Each chapter heading begins with the letter "S" as a mnemonic device to help you remember these key strands or building blocks of a vibrant spirituality. These specific themes have been chosen as a means of addressing the loss of the sense of the sacred and the destructive aspects of the dominant Western civilization in which we live. Changing values and lifestyles demand a new way of addressing age-old human struggles. Healthy spirituality is always going to be countercultural in its work of creating a life-giving environment.

Religion is a container: a system of faith, with creeds, dogmas, and means of worship. Spirituality, the "contents" of that container, is a manner of living out our belief or value system, keeping us focused on the pathway. Ideally, these two perspectives flow into and out of each other. But spirituality is much broader than any particular religion. For example, we notice the differences among Benedictine, Franciscan, Ignatian, and Carmelite spiritualties and yet all of them are Catholic in origin and practice. Given this definition, it is possible to practice a creation spirituality, a spirituality of sports, or even a business or science spirituality. What do you believe in? How are your beliefs expressed in the way you live your life? What are your core values? What gives you meaning? These are the building blocks of your spirituality. Maintaining your spirituality necessitates creating a fine balance between discipline and freedom. This book offers a way of developing, fostering, and deepening a spirituality that is soul-centered, grounded on the interior life. Consequently, I have included some very traditional as well as contemporary themes that have assisted countless numbers of people to progress in the spiritual life. Sometimes this means crossing over time-honored traditions, following the example of people like Bede Griffiths or Thomas Merton, both Catholic monks, who each in their own way turned to some Eastern practices to go deeper into their own Catholic tradition.

Spirituality is a developmental process. It is the art of making connections, seeing the Divine in the human, and claiming it for ourselves. Every day we become more human, or less human, depending upon our ability to reflect on our experiences. Some spiritualties are dangerous, in that they are attempts to somehow circumvent our finite humanity. One of the signs of a healthy spirituality is that it offers a cohesive worldview: there is a place for everything and everyone—no exclusivism. All the parts fit together—tragedy and glory, suffering and joy—and everything in between. All the pieces play a part, but not necessarily equally.

At the core of a healthy spirituality is the recognition and acceptance that reality has its limitations and connections. We affirm the limited nature of our humanity. This is an essential task for our becoming fully human. Our losses, deaths, and diminishments affirm this truth as well. A liberating spirituality must be personal and appropriate to the context of our lives. What is good for one person is not necessarily helpful to another. One size does not fit all. In speaking about the spiritual formation of adults, we must return to the basics of our faith and learn how to co-create an effective spirituality that develops over time. This book will help you do just that and more!

I

Slow Down
You're Movin' Too Fast

(Busyness/Restlessness)

MANY YEARS AGO, at one of my first parish assignments, as I was preparing to celebrate Eucharist one Sunday, I suddenly remembered that I had left my homily notes in my room. With an urgent haste that surprised me, I ran out the sacristy door and almost knocked over a small boy who was attempting to enter the sacristy. In my frustration at being "slowed down," I thought, "Get out of the way! Don't you know who I am? I'm about important business." Immediately I sensed the still inner voice of the Lord gently but firmly saying to me, "This little one is every bit as important to me as you are."

When we are in a hurry, we often lose sight of who we are in the face of Ultimate Mystery, and the essential values of our limited nature as human beings. We tend to objectify others and personify objects. This comes under the heading of idolatry—perhaps the ultimate sin—with its many faces of disguised importance. What makes this process so attractive is that it appears to be for the good, not reflecting any malice or evil intent. After all, we are only doing this good for "God" or for some other lofty purpose, when in reality we might be doing it for our own self-aggrandizement.

Spirituality is all about learning how to see, even in the darkness. When I am honest with myself as I look inside, I see a person who wants to appear kind rather than do the real work of becoming kind, one who wants to be intelligent and knowledgeable, but not do the hard study and reflection required; one who wants to seem generous, but who is actually quite self-centered. This can lead to jealousy and envy of other people's gifts. Examining my own interior life for the purpose of growth and development is a discipline that requires perspective and patient loving care. This is the difficult undertaking of acknowledging my inauthenticity and transforming it into something real and human. When I am overly busy, I lose sight of who I am and try to be someone else, an automaton, a human "doing" rather than a human "being." It is then that I feel separated from my true self and slip into living from a place of inauthenticity and self-destruction.

Thomas Merton put it well when he said, "There is a pervasive form of contemporary violence…[and that is] activism and overwork. The rush and pressure of modern life are a form, perhaps the most common form, of its innate violence. To allow oneself to be carried away by a multitude of conflicting concerns, to surrender to too many demands, to commit oneself to too many projects, to want to help everyone in everything, is to succumb to violence….It destroys our own inner capacity for peace. It destroys the fruitfulness of our own work, because it kills the root of inner wisdom which makes work fruitful" (*Conjectures of a Guilty Bystander*, 80–81).

Busyness has been referred to variously as a compulsion, an addiction, and a demon. At its core, busyness is an escape from my true self, my deepest experience of innate wisdom. This division can destroy my inner life. The Chinese have a sobering insight into this seductive work. The pictograph for *busy* is composed of two characters: *heart* and *killing*. Busyness often masks a deep restlessness that is manifested in moving from one thing to another. These are cultural wounds that can reveal themselves in mindless channel surfing, incessant shopping, compulsive eating or drinking, constant attention to cell phone messaging, and unsafe driving practices. Underneath these habits is a temptation to believe that we can do it all, or have it all, right now. This is what theologian Janet Ruffing calls a "state of mind or habit of the heart" that simply feeds the ego and fuels our own sense of self-importance. The more things we have to do for our employer, family members, friends, or communities, the more important or valuable we feel. It is a never-ending cycle. The constant, immediate use of cell phones, iPads, Twitter, and Facebook only serve to exacerbate this sense of self-importance. There is no space to reflect on the deeper questions of life, or to pause and process the meaning of the day's events or encounters. We move from one thing to another as efficient machines, not as thoughtful human beings (147–59). Perhaps that is why Francis de Sales quipped, "Hurriedness is the devil."

Whether it is the busyness of too many thoughts demanding our attention at once, the enticement of several feelings tickling our consciousness, or regularly attempting to multitask, we can lose our groundedness and our way in life. To focus on the one thought, one feeling, or one activity in front of us is the work of a life-giving spirituality. The Book of Ecclesiastes tells us, "For everything there is a season, and a time for every matter under heaven" (3:1). There is a time for work and a time for leisure, a time for action and a time for contemplation. This natural rhythm reminds us of the great and deep truths of the cosmos about right balance. Busyness is the enemy of a contemplative approach to life that invites us to view reality from a thoughtful and compassionate perspective. Without this mindfulness, we can lose this precious perspective of the moment, the project, or the person through a hurried or harried approach (Ruffing). It then becomes an endless burden to be carried, rather than a work to be created for the greater development of the human condition.

Busyness can become self-destructive when it is subconsciously used to cover feelings of discomfort (for example, feelings of loneliness, nagging life questions, or relational issues). Busyness can also be used to numb our feelings and detach us from other people, thus deepening our sense of isolation and causing us to become more mechanistic. This is one reason why different religious traditions set aside specific periods of time to pray during the day: to remind us of our higher connection to God as Ultimate Mystery and to our own human nature. This is also the source of the tradition of Sabbath rest (Ruffing).

At its core, extreme busyness separates us from our center, our true nature. This divided, distracted consciousness is perhaps the most dangerous part of an overly busy life. To counteract this tendency, Buddhism offers the daily practice of mindfulness. Christianity added the practice of regular recollection. These practices were offered as a means of puncturing the false ego, so that the true self could emerge. Who am I beyond my appointments, my connections, my duties, my titles, my roles? What I do and who I am are two separate things. We are God's breath, God's beloved, God's image. When we live from this perspective, we see ourselves, others, and reality itself differently. Again, from Thomas Merton, "The gate of heaven is everywhere." At any moment, in every encounter, we have the opportunity to enter this realm. In Christianity, this is called the reign of God, the place where the truth of God and this world intersect.

The Talmud says, "We see things as we are, not as they are," meaning we see in others what is in us—the seer and the seen are connected. So we practice seeing clearly what is really happening, by letting go of judgmentalism, which is ego-centered, and embracing a contemplative outlook, which is soul-centered. Judgmentalism is power-based while contemplative viewing is grounded in compassion. This type of viewing of reality takes place every time we observe ourselves, another person, an event or a thought, without assigning it a moral position as either good or bad, right or wrong. It is what it is. We often do this naturally when we observe babies, giving them the space just to be themselves, innocent and unaware.

The fullness of time is in this moment (*chairos*), so we are to take notice of how we live in this moment, for this is how we live every moment of our lives (Rohr, *Everything Belongs*). Are you living in the present or skipping from one experience to another with no reflection or insight? As Socrates observed, an unexamined life is not worth living. This is not one more "thing" to do but a way of living within the rhythm of nature. It is a focusing on a singularity of purpose, which is the gateway to the Divine. This is why so many saints remind us that less is better in terms of the spiritual life.

Swiss psychoanalyst Carl Jung once noted that it is not concepts that transform us, but images and symbols. One way to connect regularly with this new way of viewing the present moment is to ask ourselves throughout the day, "Am I present now?" Traditionally, many religions fostered practices of wearing a symbol to ground the religious practitioner to this truth. Nowadays this can be a personal symbol worn around the neck or kept in a pocket or in one's workspace. I know of one young man who even had a tattoo of a clock made on his upper arm to remind him to live in the present moment. What might work for you?

Another way of living life so that we respect our limitations and live with the awareness of the present moment is to integrate the three centers of mind, body, and soul. This is like building a life raft with the key components of daily physical, intellectual, emotional, and spiritual practices.

- *Physical*: choose a form of movement that celebrates your body (for example, yoga, dance, Tai Chi, Pilates, walking, exercise)
- *Intellectual*: choose a form of reading, learning, or doing something new every day as a means of enlightening yourself
- *Emotional*: choose a form of play, relational connection, or creativity that releases your inner yearning for intimate connection
- *Spiritual*: choose a prayer form or spiritual practice that fits the context of your life and yet expands your boundaries

Depending upon how busy your day is, you can adjust the amount of time that you regularly give to each of these components of your humanity. Bring your life to prayer and your prayer to the context of your life. The soul is like a sponge, in that it will receive and use whatever you give it to digest, whether it is something brief or lengthy. For example, on days when you have enough time, you might devote 30–60 minutes to each of these aspects. On days when you can only give a fleeting glance to this discipline, you might give 10–15 minutes to each component. This is an example of healthy tending to the regular needs of your personhood. Believe it or not, this will assist you in avoiding greater problems later down the track.

As Chris Cartwright, SJ, points out, our spiritual practices must always address these questions:

1. What are we serving with our lives?
2. What are we striving for?

3. What do we judge to be important, and value?
4. What are we doing with our love and our yearning for love?

Spirituality is a practice, a way to remain faithful to love. Those practices that most enable us to remain faithful to love are the practices that reflect our desire to act on the word of God heard in the depths of our heart.

Here are some ways of getting you started or encouraging you on your way. You might ask yourself one or more of these to "jumpstart" your own creativity.

QUESTIONS

Is it enough for me to just be?

What thoughts, feelings fill my interior space at this time?

What will satisfy me?

How do I focus on this moment?

PRAYER FORMS

Theological reflection: An exercise of "looking back" over the day's activities, seeking to discover meaning, or the presence of God in those events or encounters. Generally, three steps are involved: Experience, Reflection, and Response.

Jesus Prayer: A traditional Eastern Orthodox repetitive prayer originating in the "internal speaking" of the name of Jesus by the fourth- and fifth-century desert fathers and mothers. Sometimes this prayer is accompanied by the use of beads.

SPIRITUAL PRACTICES

Siesta: A specific time of relaxation or "time out" that could involve a nap, light reading, or conversation.

Tai Chi: A Chinese form of martial art practiced for both its defense training and its health benefits. There are a multitude of training forms, both traditional and contemporary, that offer a slow, gentle form of exercise that involves full-body movement.

Sabbath rest: A specific time set aside to abstain from work and focus on leisure and prayer.

Mindfulness of thought, feeling, behavior, and choices: A Buddhist practice of consciously focusing on the moment, with full awareness and intention.

Contemplative walk: A slow, deliberate pace of walking that focuses on the movement and not the goal or distance covered.

FURTHER READING

May, Gerald. *Care of Mind, Care of Spirit.* San Francisco: Harper San Francisco, 1982.

Muller, Wayne. *Sabbath: Finding Rest, Renewal, and Delight in Our Busy Lives.* New York: Bantam Books, 1999.

Pennington, M. Basil. *Centered Living: The Way of Centering Prayer.* New York: Doubleday, 1988.

Rolheiser, Ronald. *The Shattered Lantern: Rediscovering a Felt Presence of God.* New York: Crossroad, 2005.

2

Solitude
Leave Me Alone

(Loneliness/Negativity)

SR. MARY JOSE HOBDAY tells the story of a day when she was a young girl at home on the Native American reservation. She was, by her own admission, acting in a perfectly cantankerous manner, with no desire to change her attitude or her actions. Her father ordered her to grab a book, an apple, and a blanket, and to meet him in the car. Slowly and grudgingly, she made her way to the car, where her father waited in silence for her. They drove for a while, in continued silence, to a nearby canyon, where he stopped the vehicle and ordered her out, with the words, "I'll be back late this afternoon." With that, he drove off in a cloud of dust. In her anger, she threw the apple over the cliff and sat down on the blanket feeling very alone, frustrated, and self-righteous in her negative attitude. As time went by, however, she began to calm down and was able to observe her surroundings. She climbed down the face of the cliff to find her apple and sat down to read for a bit. Eventually, she put down her book and simply sat and looked. The beautiful vista, the quiet, and the emptiness worked on her in such a way that her mood began to change, as she opened up her soul to the wider mystery of who and where she was. Later, when her father came to collect her, her mood had changed completely. She felt much better and realized that she had just learned a very important life lesson: solitude is the antidote to loneliness and interior discomfort. Her father never pressured her to talk about her experience, but those around her experienced the clear difference in her (Bausch, 170–71).

No matter how many friends we have or how gregarious we are, we all face moments, days, or even long periods of loneliness. This is a reality within marriage, family, community, society. Loneliness is neither a curse, nor a sign that something is wrong with us. Rather, loneliness is a form of impoverishment that invites us to a deeper self-knowledge and interior engagement. Solitude is the antidote to loneliness. It is here in this place of "chosen aloneness" that we re-encounter the gift and beauty of our fullness and individuality. All we need can be found within us. Everything is a reflection of that interior life. Beauty, goodness, peace, and even their opposites, ugliness, evil, and violence, are all present within each one of us. To pay adequate attention to this constellation of themes without becoming overwhelmed, we must face our feelings and thoughts, not as victims, but as objective observers. French saint Thérèse of Lisieux said it this way, "Whoever is willing to serenely bear the trial of being displeasing to oneself is a pleasant place for Jesus to dwell." This is hard, active work, demanding effort, but it bears great rewards. In the Book of Genesis (2:15), we read that Adam worked with God in caring for the Garden of Eden. We, too, are invited to work with God in caring for the garden of our soul, that it may bear the fruit of a virtuous life.

During one particularly lonely time in my life, I found solace in giving voice to my feelings in the form of a poem I wrote in my journal:

Loneliness—friend or foe?

I dare say I do not know which you are.
At times you frighten me and envelope me in your cold,
    grasping claws, taking my breath away,
    my very life.
There is no joy around you, no life, no happiness.
All appears gloomy in your presence.
Blinded by the darkness of your oppression, I lose my taste for life.
And yet the many hours that I have spent in the counsel of your lap
    have taught me numerous things. Not least among them are
    these:

Look deeply, be aware, observe, be patient, and at peace, trust life
    and live the present moment fully…
You are indeed the harshest of all teachers but the wisest I've
    ever known.
For, Loneliness, when you are turned inside out you become:
Solitude—my friend.

What is the message underneath the feeling, or the emotion behind
the thought? Loneliness is often experienced as "being out of sorts" or
being negative. All behavior is need-directed. It remains then, for us to discern the real message behind the negative feeling or behavior. For this
reason, and for the sake of our own happiness, we need to become our
own "meteorologist" and objectively monitor the emotional weather
patterns of our interior life and respond from a grounded, centered
place. Reject the temptation of becoming a victim to your own incessant,
tortured thoughts, feelings, or repetitive behavior. This is the work of a
poet, an artist, and a mature human being.

    In twelve-step work, recovering addicts are encouraged to be ruthlessly
honest with themselves and their patterns of thought, feeling, and behavior. One helpful technique, expressed in the acronym HALT, consists of this
mandate: Never let yourself become too Hungry, Angry, Lonely, or Tired.
One of my friends likes to add Hurried and Horny to his list. These are the
times when we can often slip into our own preferred forms of self-
destructive, negative behaviors, all the while blaming the rest of the world
for our problems. Nothing changes unless something changes. What needs
to change when you encounter your own times of HALT?

    These stress points, common to most human beings, can cause any of
us to fall prey to our own demons. Notice that loneliness is listed here
as a reminder that we are social creatures; when we are not in right relationship with ourselves or other people, we will seek out unhealthy ways
and means of "hooking up" or "connecting." One of the fastest growing
avenues for doing just this—both physically and emotionally—is online
pornography. What can we learn from the wisdom of those who have
suffered so much from their own loneliness and self-absorption? Choose
to act before being acted upon by reality! Seek out and recognize

moments of solitude and reflection. Choose consciously to do just one thing at a time. Layman Pang, a renowned Buddhist practitioner, once said, "When you walk, walk, when you wash, wash, when you chop wood, chop wood." Such focused attention defies the cultural practice of maximizing one's time by doing several things at once. This has the deleterious effect of dividing ourselves into separate compartments, one of the most dangerous situations in the spiritual life.

The ultimate work of spirituality is about communion and unity, not separation and division. Choosing specific times of solitude as an energizing and life-giving practice is a necessary component of a healthy adult life. As philosopher Albert Camus said, "In order to understand the world, one has to turn away from it on occasion." Whether it is spending time alone with your thoughts and feelings in the comfort of your home, or going to a local park or wilderness site, solitude can reward us with a greater sense of interior comfort and acceptance of reality as it is. Solitude offers us a clarifying perspective. The amount of time commitment depends upon the individual context of one's life and the issues that present themselves for attention.

In Mark 1:29–39, we read about the way in which Jesus responds to the busyness of village life and to expectations and requests that threaten to overwhelm his ministry. "In the morning, while it was still very dark, he got up and went out to a deserted place, and there he prayed." This time of solitude and active engagement with his interior life was essential for Jesus, as we discover in the lines that follow this comment. Peter and his companions seek Jesus out, insisting he come back and continue his good work. They are delighting in the reflected glory of Jesus' fame and want to maintain their status and honor in this community. But Jesus has experienced, in his solitude time, a reconnection with his deepest self, and found his center in his relationship with Abba. Thus fortified, he is able to courageously move against the expectations of his beloved disciples and follow his inner voice. We see this happening regularly and often in the life of Christ.

It has been said that it is not the bad things that get in the way of our life's work; rather it is the many good things, and the expectations of others that act as temptations to pull us away from the inner promptings of the Spirit. How true this is! Quiet time, meditation, or reflection, call it what you want—this is what makes us human and makes life worth living—learning and growing from our choices. Solitude is merely the conscious delivery system that enables this process to happen.

QUESTIONS

What situations or occasions generally seem to engender feelings of loneliness for you?

How do you normally respond to loneliness?

What have you learned from your times of solitude?

PRAYER FORMS

Meditation: A form of prayer that involves quiet reflection on a sacred text, image, or music.

Prayer of gratitude: A specific way of giving thanks for some favor received, prayer answered, or reality accepted.

Journaling: A conversational means of prayer that involves writing and dialogue with God, others, or parts of oneself.

Praying the psalms or writing your own: Reading or singing the psalms as communal prayer forms or writing your own individual expression of human longing.

SPIRITUAL PRACTICES

Sit or wander in nature: Observe nature, both in the large view and from the smaller perspective through strolling, hiking, or sitting in the midst of a park or wilderness.

Do volunteer work: Offering your time or expertise to individuals or organizations working to better society.

Reach out to someone in need: Connecting with others through a specific need develops friendships and builds community.

Make a retreat: This consists of time spent away from our usual environment for a half day, a day, or a week.

FURTHER READING

Brueggemann, Walter. *The Message of the Psalms: A Theological Commentary.* Minneapolis: Augsburg, 1984.

Finley, James. *Christian Meditation: Experiencing the Presence of God.* San Francisco: Harper San Francisco, 2004.

Kelsey, Morton. *Adventure Inward: Christian Growth through Personal Journal Writing.* Minneapolis: Augsburg, 1980.

Rolheiser, Ronald. *The Restless Heart: Finding Our Spiritual Home in Times of Loneliness.* New York: Doubleday, 2004.

3

Sacrifice
Offer It Up

(Laziness/Loss of Awe and Wonder)

WHEN I WAS A LITTLE BOY, whenever something didn't go my way, or when I got hurt, my mother would always say, "Offer it up." I didn't quite understand the depth of this maternal wisdom until years later. But in effect, she was saying, "Don't waste your time wallowing in self-pity. Let it go. Move on. Give it to God."

To truly sacrifice something, anything, is to offer it up for something greater. The word *sacrifice* comes from the Latin word meaning "to make holy." A holy life is one that regularly seeks out the greater by letting go of the smaller—viewpoint, situation, or past memory. To live well as a human being involves sacrificing often. This does not mean that the process has to look or feel holy. Rather, to sacrifice means to let go of one's attachment to comfort and reach out to help another person or improve a situation, thus viewing life from a different perspective. Examples: parents who lovingly care for a disabled child or grandparents who babysit their grandchildren while their single parent goes to work, or a busy executive who volunteers his or her time to tutor inner city children in reading. These are channels of enlarging one's heart and mind. This is the disciplined work of attention to one's interior life and to the needs of others. This is the antithesis of laziness or a self-centered approach to reality.

Sacrificing is a means of cutting back the weeds of our interior garden in order that we might more clearly see the real beauty of life. One of the benefits of the aging process is that we begin to notice this truth more often. Yes, life slows us down but we see more clearly. We may do fewer things, but with more attention and understanding of the meaning of it all. Grandchildren are a wonderful gift in this process and can be reminders of what is most important in life.

One of the great endowments that young children can give adults is the ever-new blessing of awe and wonder about reality. Whether it is the awe of animals, or wonder of a flower, or the delight in bubbles, children help us tap into our inner child. Sometimes in our overly rational approach to reality, we can lose our connection to wonder and amazement and thus we, in a sense, lose our way in the cosmos. Entrapment in bitterness, cynicism, or an overly rationalistic approach to life, can lead to a calcified state of existence. Laughter and tears, which come so easily and frequently to children, are often forgotten and neglected by adults. Tears occur when the soul experiences the pain of life, while laughter blossoms when the soul sees the absurdity of life. To laugh and weep often is a good sign of a healthy soul, an embodied sign of offering up the situation and letting it go, like a floating bubble.

That which is truly sacrificed to God becomes glorified or transformed. The biblical story of Job is a good model for us as we grapple with our suffering and lament our losses. Job sat with his overwhelming losses, weeping and lamenting, crying out to God, demanding an explanation. Yet God gave Job no explanation, no consoling reason for his undeserved suffering, only God's own presence in the darkness. Sometimes we must even let go of our need to understand why things happen the way they do. Reality, in the end, is itself our best teacher.

Carl Jung pointed out that because we are not willing to face the legitimate suffering in life, we create our own form of neurotic suffering. Legitimate suffering is that which seeks meaning. Because Job willed himself to remain in the cauldron of oppositional truths—holding onto the reality of his pain and at the same time acknowledging his continued trust in a just God—he was transformed, finding meaning in his suffering. Job's suffering moved him to consciousness and an honest relationship with God, so much so that he was instructed to teach his religiously stifled, and misguided friends.

There is no God experience without some type of surrender; and here is the paradox. We are to surrender to God (offer up, turn over, let go) and at the same time take responsibility for our own life without blaming others. This is the central understanding of the twelve-step programs that are so popular among recovering addicts, alcoholics, and other compulsively oriented individuals. This is also the core of the paschal mystery, the central theme of Christianity. The Carmelite mystic, John of the Cross, said it this way: The language of God is the experience of our lives. God works with us through the reality of our lives.

Everything comes to an end. How do we face or accept this truth? Christianity shows us the way through a solemn five-step process that is honored liturgically. Theologian Ronald Rolheiser puts it succinctly:

1. Good Friday: life is lost (honoring, accepting the pain and tragedy of reality); the response is a pondering process of letting the pain teach you.
2. Easter Sunday: reception of new life (walk through the pain to the other side of something brand new, different); the response is celebration.
3. Forty days: grieving and adjusting to a new reality (letting go process); the response is shadow work, forgiveness.
4. Ascension: refusal to cling to the old life (learning life's lessons on its own terms); the response is letting the old life bless us in a new way that we might become a blessing to others.
5. Pentecost: reception of the new Spirit for the new life that one is already living (courage to be authentic, human); the response is sharing and connecting with others (146–48).

This ongoing process teaches us that salvation is not pain, sin, or negativity avoided but rather, faced and overcome (Rohr, *Falling Upward*, 60). This is the sacrificial work of the individual, the community—the work of becoming whole, holy. Indeed this is the painful but necessary work of transformation. Without this conscious work, one suffers in extra measure and without meaning.

Some religious traditions speak about an ascetical or disciplined approach to life that helps a person to address the disordered or disproportionate aspects of life. This may include certain penances, choices, lifestyle changes, or therapeutic work. At the core of living a balanced life is a profound respect for the human person and for human limitations. Therefore, the choice of particular contemporary ascetical practices must be based upon an individual's interior needs, not what looks good to others. Some means of self-discipline might include:

- Regular fasting
- Abstinence from a particular type of food or drink or activity for a short or long period
- Avoidance of gossip or negative talking
- Cultivation of virtues
- Living a simple lifestyle
- Commitment to forgiveness
- Supporting a favorite charity or cause with time and/or money
- Resolving relational conflicts as quickly as possible
- Letting go of undue attachments

Living with a disciplined, sacrificial attitude involves facing reality on its own terms without taking things personally or blaming others. It is to live consciously with particular choices, actions, and practices that artfully shape our lives into a beautiful mosaic.

QUESTIONS

What do you need to let go of or offer up to God?

What are you learning from the experience of your own life?

How do you respond to tragedy, global suffering, the overwhelming suffering of the human condition?

How might you integrate a sacrificial attitude/practice into your life?

PRAYER FORMS

Ritual: An embodied expression of one's deep desire to transition through to something new.

Charles de Foucauld's Prayer of Abandonment: A "desert" prayer offering oneself completely and confidently to God.

Prayer of Saint Francis: A traditional Franciscan peace prayer.

Serenity Prayer: A simple prayer of sobriety used by twelve-step groups (not just for sobriety).

SPIRITUAL PRACTICES

Daily discipline of prayer, exercise, play, and study (PEPS): A means of honoring and strengthening all aspects of our humanity.

Real presence: Bringing the fullness of one's essence and attention to a relationship or encounter. This is the true self.

Shadow work: The humble, honest acceptance and integration of one's underappreciated interior components, perhaps unknown, in the work of becoming whole.

Celebration: This can include dancing, singing, free-form movement, games, and festive meals.

Contemporary asceticism: Specific practices that are focused upon unhealthy or unhelpful aspects of one's life. The goal is to bring into proper balance that which is out of alignment with one's value system (for example, choosing to eat less sugar to improve one's health, or choosing less online time with IT devices for more time with one's interior life).

Forgiveness: A specific practice of letting go of past blockages to experience a new beginning. This involves three steps: (1) Acknowledge the hurt or irritation; (2) Work through the resentment; (3) Choose to forgive.

Contemplative stance: A spacious way of observing reality non-judgmentally (for example, a slow walk in nature, gazing at a picture of a loved one, observing your thoughts or feelings in a detached manner).

FURTHER READING

Clarke, Jim. *Creating Rituals: A New Way of Healing for Everyday Life.* New York/Mahwah, NJ: Paulist Press, 2010.

Funk, Mary Margaret. *Tools Matter for Practicing the Spiritual Life.* New York: Continuum, 2001.

Miller, William. *Make Friends with Your Shadow: How to Accept and Use Positively the Negative Side of Your Personality.* Minneapolis: Augsburg, 1981.

Stoop, David. *Forgiving the Unforgivable.* Ann Arbor, MI: Servant Publications, 2003.

4

Saints
I Want to Be in That Number

(Isolation/Self-absorption)

ONE OF THE MOST BEAUTIFUL and striking features of the Catholic Cathedral of Our Lady of the Angels in Los Angeles are the tapestries of artist John Nava. Like a dual procession along the sides of the nave, over 130 saints of all ages and historical periods appear as contemporary men and women in their own individual cultural dress. Each saint stands in a relaxed, dignified pose, looking toward the sanctuary, rather than at the viewer. This array of images, stunning in its originality and emotive power, honors the multicultural reality of the Los Angeles Archdiocese and reminds the viewer that we are a global, trans-historical Church. It also invites the viewer to recognize that these are ordinary human beings, not gods, with their own stories of faith and courage. Finally and perhaps most important, several *unnamed* individuals in the tapestries invite the viewer to take his or her rightful place and join in the procession of saints, mystics, and prophets. The first time I entered the cathedral and walked down the main aisle, I felt energized and encouraged in my own life story by these holy people of God. It was a memorable experience of being moved by this powerful symbol.

The artist Robert Irwin's words, carved in stone in the J. P. Getty Museum Garden in Los Angeles, capture for many the experience of God and great-minded, holy people: "Ever present, never twice the same; Ever changing, never less than whole." Holiness is, to a certain extent, unique to each individual. When we completely open ourselves to this mystery of love, wholeness happens, but never in quite the same way as anywhere else. This great mystery reminds us that all human beings are invited to follow the dictum of the prophet Micah, announced over three thousand years ago:

> He has told you, O mortal, what is good;
>> and what does the LORD require of you
> but to do justice, and to love kindness,
>> and to walk humbly with your God?
>>>> (6:8)

Micah's threefold challenge describes the spiritual life as a journey inward (prayer), outward (charity), and forward (justice). To become fully human is the task of every individual. To grow in one's unique beingness is perhaps the most challenging task for each of us. Teilhard de Chardin, the great Jesuit paleontologist and theologian, puts it this way, "We are not human beings having a spiritual experience; we are spiritual beings having a human experience."

Every culture as well as every religion has stories of heroes and heroines that hold up for us humans this process of living out the heroic ideals and virtues of a people. Great-minded people, motivated by exemplary ideals, the kingdom, the betterment of community, or the environment, show us the way. For example, Jesus discovered his divinity in the transcendent depths of his humanity, and so it is with us. God grows in us as we grow with God. God acts and is acted upon. We are already spiritual by virtue of the Creator; our life's work is to become whole, fully human. This is difficult, messy work. Jesus models this for us, as does every saint or holy person.

As long as our models of holiness are held above us, we will remain small and mediocre in our approach to human development. When we understand these models as personal invitations and encouragements extended to us, we will grow in our own transformation process. No one matures in isolation. It is in the day-to-day interactions with other people that we really discover who we are, and what needs changing. Pseudo-intimacy is no replacement for the authentic work of emotional engagement. This is one of the great temptations of the social networking movement—to replace real conversation with messaging and call it a relationship.

With the death of Christendom—the cluster of social structures that framed and enabled the socialization in and transmission of Christian beliefs, values, and practices in families, communities, and nations—and even the waning of Catholic tribal loyalty, we face a new and sometimes frightening reality: we are still responsible for our own spiritual growth. In this scenario, perhaps more than ever before, saints and communities are offered as inspiration and support on our journey as we develop our own styles of transformative prayer and energizing spiritualties. This is one reason why particular individuals or communities attract us. For example, women of a particular personality and spirituality will be drawn to the determined and feisty Mary MacKillop, others of a more pious disposition will find inspiration in someone like Thérèse of Lisieux. Similarly, affinities with Francis of Assisi or Thomas Aquinas will prove beneficial to some, and not others. Spiritual friendships often develop between likeminded people who are serious about their growth in faith. Witness the many spiritual friendships that have enlivened the pages of Church history (Francis and Clare of Assisi, Teresa of Avila and John of the Cross, Francis de Sales and Jane de Chantal).

Unfortunately, we are often tempted to choose the numbing way of comfort rather than the vital and necessary road of transformation. Many ecclesial leaders and communities focus primarily on fostering devotional prayers and practices that provide no real hope of conversion or transformation. The great saints moved beyond these comforting practices to works of justice and peacemaking. Here we have it again: the journey inward, outward, and forward. Prayer is authenticated by reaching out in works of charity and justice; otherwise, it becomes another form of narcissistic comfort.

Saints help us to move away from a sense of isolation and self-absorption to a regular immersion practice of involvement in reality. One retired woman I know found a way to connect her faith with her desire to help others by participating in a weekly soup kitchen and community garden. The gift given became the gift received when she discovered that she received much more from the homeless then she had ever thought possible.

Saints come from every walk of society. Most are not canonized (a lengthy and involved ecclesial process) and many have been in conflict with Church leaders. These self-actualized men and women regularly are considered unorthodox and unacceptable because their great love of God and human beings overrode all other considerations. Their focus is not necessarily on propriety or the ecclesial niceties expected of the "holy ones of God." Saints exhibit many different missions and spiritualties in their lives because of their unique encounters with God. This is their driving force. How do you know someone is holy? One woman put it this way, "I know my friend is holy because I feel holy when I am around her." Holiness begets holiness and bears the undeniable fruit of the Spirit.

"You shall be holy, for I the LORD your God am holy" (Lev 19:2b). How are you growing in wholeness/holiness?

QUESTIONS

Which saints' stories "grab" you and encourage you?

Who are your heroines/heroes?

Where are you being invited to step more deeply into your unique humanity?

PRAYER FORMS

Litany: A devotional form of prayer consisting of a series of petitions addressed to God or to a particular saint, prayed individually or in community.

Novena: An institutional form of devotion that consists of specific private or public prayers repeated over a period of nine days. These prayers are often dedicated to a specific angel, saint, or to the Blessed Virgin Mary, seeking specific graces.

Intercessory prayer: Praying for a particular person or intention.

Adapting a prayer form of a particular saint: Contextualizing a specific prayer to one's life (for example, meditating on the Scriptures by imagining oneself in the story of St. Ignatius of Loyola).

SPIRITUAL PRACTICES

Connecting positively with intimate friends: Visits, holidays, gatherings, phone calls, healthy use of social networking—texting, e-mail, Skype/Facetime, or Facebook.

Reading the lives of saints/heroes: Learning from people in history who have modeled for us goodness and integrity.

Art pieces, holy cards: Visual reminders of greatness and the best of humanity.

Iconography: Invitations to step into the Divine Presence through the contemplation or creation of icons.

Fostering healthy relationships: Working to improve my Emotional Quotient and relational abilities.

Honoring otherness: Talking to others who come from a cultural background different from your own or who share a different spiritual tradition.

FURTHER READING

Ellsberg, Robert, ed. *Modern Spiritual Masters: Writings on Contemplation and Compassion.* Maryknoll, NY: Orbis Books, 2008.

Flinders, Carol Lee. *Enduring Grace: Living Portraits of Seven Women Mystics.* New York: HarperCollins, 2006.

Johnson, Elizabeth. *Truly Our Sister: A Theology of Mary in the Communion of Saints.* New York: Continuum, 2003.

Martin, James. *My Life with the Saints.* Chicago: Loyola Press, 2006.

5

Sense of Humor
That's a Good One!

(Religious Rigidity/Disconnection)

JUST FOR FUN, LET ME BEGIN with a joke. Terri asked her fourth grade Sunday school class to draw pictures of their favorite Bible stories. She was puzzled by Kyle's picture, which showed four people on an airplane. So she asked him which story it was meant to represent. "The flight to Egypt," he said excitedly. Terri said, "I see. And that must be Mary, Joseph, and baby Jesus. But who is the fourth person?" "Oh, that's Pontius—the pilot." Children have a wonderful way of looking at the world.

Within Christian circles there is a tradition that in the early Church people would often tell jokes during Easter week. This was a way of reminding each other that God had the last laugh on Satan in his victory over sin and death. However, often in religious circles and among religious people, a sense of humor, joy, and laughter have gone missing. Spanish mystic Teresa of Avila once purportedly said, "God save us from dour-faced Christians!" She went on to say to a religious woman, "If you believe in Jesus, would you please inform your face!" While we cannot be naïve about human suffering and evil, we must never lose perspective on the fullness of reality. A healthy sense of humor recalls that the work of salvation is a cooperative effort with God and God invites us to trust that divine perspective.

Evil always chooses a disguise. This is what makes evil so insidious. Historically there has been much emphasis on what has been called the "hot sins" of humanity, such as sexual sins, sins of anger or violence, and sins of envy and greed. However, the "cold sins" of judgmentalism, self-centeredness, militant ignorance, hubris, and mean-spiritedness are often much more dangerous in their lasting effects on the human community. Of course we must creatively and firmly oppose evil in all its many disguises and at all levels of reality, including systemic evil, but this is no excuse for an underdeveloped sense of humor—the absence of which can provide fertile ground for those "cold" sins.

Truly spiritual people have a well-developed sense of humor. This is what makes them believable, attractive, and balanced. A good sense of humor lightens the load and reminds us not to take ourselves so seriously. Teilhard de Chardin once said, "Joy is the most infallible sign of the presence of God." Most of us miss the humor in the Sacred Scriptures of any religion because we are not reading them in the original language, or within the cultural context of the time (see 1 Kgs 18:20–28). Ecclesiastes 3:4 reminds us that there is a time for laughter. The one who cannot laugh is a fool. Laughter comes from the "shadow" or neglected side of our personality. Thus, our sense of humor is unique to us as individuals.

The private and public moral dilemmas that we wrestle with remind us that we and reality are not perfect. There is a flaw in all aspects of creation—that is how the light of the Creator gets in! (Leonard Cohen, "Anthem"). Feelings of helplessness and hopelessness can stifle us. It is most helpful to approach these issues with a mixture of humor and humility; otherwise, we can become trapped in bitterness, anger, and hubris.

Religious rigidity, at any level (personal, political, or ecclesial), is about control, not spirituality. This type of attitude uses religion as a mechanism to mercilessly control or judge others. The scapegoating of others at different levels (for example, racism, judgmentalism, nationalism) is another disguised form of evil that feeds on "either/or" thinking. Unfortunately, it has become an accepted form of sanitized violence.

If evil often presents itself in disguise, how can we discern its presence? Moral evil is known by its fruits:

- An arrogant sense of certainty with no self-doubt
- Total absence of self-criticism, only self-absorption

- A controlling attitude; there is no freedom
- Militant ignorance
- Protection of self-esteem at all costs
- Pathological narcissism
- Egocentricity
- A policy of trading in fear
- Denial of one's shadow side, often projected onto others
- An attitude destructive of life in all forms

The worst moral evil is done by unconscious people who are disconnected from their instinctual feelings. Witness the many clergy and religious elite who have fallen into violent, criminal behavior. What better place to hide from God and things authentic than in religious settings? It is much more attractive to *feel* holy and good than to *be* holy and good.

Part of the work of growing in holiness is developing a real spirit of joy, laughter, and humor in one's life, especially in the face of suffering, death, and evil. British author Margaret Silf recounts the story of two friends whose mutual friend had died. They wanted to honor the beauty of her life so they planted what they thought were daffodil bulbs on her grave and grieved all winter for their loss. In the spring, when they returned to the grave, they discovered a brilliant crop of onions! They laughed until they cried. A sense of humor grounds us and connects us to reality. It reminds us that we are not God, and that the foibles and inconsistencies of life and human beings all play a part in the story of reality. To be truly alive means to play an active role in this reality, this time and place. Humor is our response to this interaction.

A sense of humor speaks volumes about our interior life. Laughter releases the tension in our bodies and spirits and helps us experience the larger picture of reality. It reconnects us and grounds us in our humanity. At the same time, your humor is fueled and delivered by the shadow side of your personality. This is why there is so much laughter, and so many jokes at funerals, weddings, and other official functions. The shadow is at play. The shadow despises hubris and pomposity and so seeks it out to dismantle it and tame it. The shadow is the place of real instinctual power and therefore must be addressed with respect and awareness. Otherwise, it can become dark and destructive personally and communally.

Jokes are a means of deflating the ego, just as mirth lightens the mood or situation. There is an old story told about a young man who entered a strict monastery. On the first day, the abbot informed the novice that he would be allowed to speak only two words every five years. After the first five years, the novice was called into the abbot's office for his review. The abbot informed him that he was happy with his participation in the community and his contribution to the overall morale of the community. "Do you have anything to say for yourself?" asked the abbot. The monk replied, "Food cold." "Well, I'm sorry to hear that," said the abbot. Five years later the monk returns for his interview. "Okay," the abbot said, "you have been here for ten years now. What do you have to say?" The monk solemnly replied, "Bed hard." The abbot responded, "I will see what we can do about that." After five more years, the two met again. "You have been here for fifteen years. What two words would you like to say?" asked the abbot. "I quit," said the monk. "Well, I am not surprised," replied the abbot, "You have been complaining for the last fifteen years!" May you uncover the joy, laughter, and humor in life and share it with others.

QUESTIONS

What makes you laugh/cry?

Where in your own life do you notice the stirrings of evil or evil inclinations?

How do you respond to human evil?

How can you improve your sense of humor?

PRAYER FORMS

Music: Regularly listening to, or playing, any music that lifts the spirit.

Real-life language prayer: Pray from your emotions, your instincts.

SPIRITUAL PRACTICES

Dance: Let your inner music move you to proclaim your physicality.

Laughter: Seek out ways and means to laugh heartily without damage to others.

Celebrations: Take the opportunity to create ordinary celebrations with an extraordinary flair (for example, "unbirthdays," Monday mornings, Christmas in July, picnics, breakfast in bed).

Smile often: Seek out the positive in life; practice the virtue of joy.

FURTHER READING

Hughes, Gerard W. *God of Surprises*. London: Darton, Longman and Todd, 1985.

Linn, Dennis, Sheila Fabricant Linn, Matthew Linn. *Good Goats: Healing Our Image of God*. New York/Mahwah, NJ: Paulist Press, 1994.

Martin, James. *Between Heaven and Mirth: Why Joy, Humor, and Laughter Are at the Heart of the Spiritual Life*. New York: HarperCollins, 2011.

Pollard, Miriam. *The Laughter of God: At Ease with Prayer*. Wilmington, DE: Michael Glazier, 1986.

6

Service
How May I Help You?
(Narcissism/Exceptionalism)

DEVELOPMENTAL PSYCHOLOGISTS have theorized that one of the cultural signs that a boy has become a man is when he finally realizes that his life is not about himself—it's about serving others. (The development of girls has a more relational pattern). The question is not, are you having fun yet? Rather it is, how may I help? Reaching out to those in need reminds us that we are all connected, and that ultimately we need each other. St. Vincent de Paul once said, "After you have helped someone in need, thank them for the privileges of that service, for you have experienced Christ in the encounter." What a wonderful image of God, a God in need who also responds to our needs through others.

At St. John's Seminary in California, we have instituted a summer immersion program, named after St. Martin de Porres (1579–1639), the Dominican who lovingly and selflessly cared for the forgotten, rejected members of the Peruvian society in which he lived. In this thirty-day experience, the seminarians are given the opportunity to not only interact with the poor, but also to experience their own inner poverty. It has been a transformative experience for them. One identified the program as "the best experience I have had as a seminarian." "I finally understand," he said, "what real ministry is—a face-to-face encounter with human need and misery, in the form of authentic presence."

One of the dominant themes of American culture is individualism, where choices and options override commitment and community. Years ago, the French political thinker and historian Alexis de Tocqueville pointed this out, saying that what makes America great is its individualistic spirit, and yet this will be its downfall. De Tocqueville's prophetic insight is now apparent in several areas of U.S. society: the rapid decline of active membership in volunteer organizations, the increase in destruction and defacing of public property, and the increasing imbalance between individual rights and communal well-being. Large numbers of Americans have lost sight of the need to serve others. Without a regular conscious practice of serving others, along with a consciousness of the larger picture, we can easily get lost in a self-serving, narcissistic grandiosity that can only lead to more divisiveness and destruction.

The thinking pattern often follows along these or similar lines:

1. I would like....
2. I need....
3. I deserve....
4. It's my right to....
5. It's mine!

Notice the commercials on television and in other media. They regularly follow this pattern, and in the process earn higher and higher revenues by tapping successfully into this self-serving way of thinking. This thought process then moves itself into an attitudinal shift of exceptionalism, which, in turn, leads to a behavioral change that narrows the focus of our attention. Service, on the other hand, opens up our own little world to see and experience reality as God sees it: we are all related. As Michael Graham, SJ, reflects, "Service is what prayer looks like when it gets up off its knees and walks around in the world."

The work of liberating spirituality is practicing sharing in family, community, and culture, crossing linguistic, economic, and national boundaries. In a nutshell, it's about right relationship and connection. For this reason, many mystics across the religious spectrum speak about a communion with the Divine that is translated into an active communal service to others. As

Blessed Teresa of Calcutta has accurately pointed out, the reason we have poverty is because we have forgotten that we belong to each other. Poverty expresses itself in many forms: mental illness, physical disability, economic hardship, homelessness, social ineptitude, emotional incongruities, and so on. Which type of poverty most discomfits you? Spiritual writer and activist Jean Vanier learned much from his L'Arche communities in serving the "nobodies" of the world. His example, and that of others like him, can teach us plenty. For example, many people are afraid of the poor or disadvantaged, or have incorrect perceptions of poverty. Service with and for the poor can correct misconceptions and redirect our energies in a more meaningful way—the way of compassion.

Many years ago, as part of my education in clinical pastoral care, I was assigned as chaplain to Morningside Convalescent Home in New York, which specialized in caring for Alzheimer patients. One day I encountered a man named Adam, who was in the late stages of the disease. Adam was exceptional for several reasons. His head was shaved, and he was restrained in a wheelchair, unable to say even one intelligible word in any language. Twice I approached him, but I was so frightened that I left immediately. The following week I returned and encountered Adam's wife. Through her, I learned surprisingly, that Adam was a robust ninety-three-year-old former athlete, an internationally educated and linguistically gifted man. He was being restrained because he was so strong. He had recently pulled out two teeth and tufts of his own hair. Over time, I befriended this couple, and in the process, confronted my own fear of mental illness. Near the end of my time at the home, I finally was ready to accept the gift that Adam had unceremoniously offered me: my own fear of losing my memory, or even my mind. Before I left my ministry there, I went one day to the chapel and presented myself to the Lord, offering up my memory, my intelligence, and my education. Through this humble offering, I truly felt transformed, reconnected, and grounded.

Creation has a natural rhythm and balance; healthy spirituality does as well. When your reality is in conflict with the creative balance of the universe, then you are looking at a toxic spirituality. The transcendent focus must always be grounded by the material world. For example, if a person has an excessive preoccupation with passive devotional practices with no outreach to social justice or works of charity, then it is self-serving, not serving God. God is personal, but never private. Worship and service are inseparable in a life-giving spirituality. Faith comes alive when we put it to work in the world. Privatized religion is another form of narcissism, as is seeking systems of moral superiority. In Luke 16:19–31, we notice that the only thing that the rich man did wrong was to ignore the obvious needs of Lazarus, the poor man at his doorstep. How you see/hear determines what you will see/hear. Jesus heard that he was the Beloved, so wherever he looked, he saw the beloved nature of others. His hearing affected his vision.

How might we serve others? Essentially, there are three categories of service:

1. *Direct aid*, such as feeding the hungry, visiting the imprisoned, caring for the sick, welcoming the stranger or foreigner
2. *Indirect aid*, such as sharing of skills, talents, knowledge, or making contacts to assist others in moving forward in life
3. *Social advocacy*, such as voter registration, working to change unjust laws, letter writing to civil or religious authorities

The task, especially for the busy person, is to choose one category and focus on one activity that can assist you in connecting your faith to your spirituality. Do your best, then, to support the other avenues of service through verbal encouragement or financial donations. In this way, you are approaching the task of service in a well-rounded way.

What type of worship do you think Jesus desires? A eucharistic approach to life teaches us that every so often we must take our own life into our hands, let it be broken open, lifted up, and shared with others, that we might be led to liberation. As we serve others, we in turn experience liberation and fulfillment, for worship and service go together.

QUESTIONS

How do you translate your faith into action in caring for the poor and disadvantaged of society?

How do you respond to your own sense of inner powerlessness or limitations?

What have you learned about yourself in your reactions to the stranger, foreigner, or poor person?

PRAYER FORMS

Liturgical celebrations: Participate in ecclesial gatherings of communal prayer.

Prayer groups: Join a prayer group centered on a particular devotion or theme.

Small faith community: Create and/or participate in a small group of like-minded believers.

Scripture reading: Read the Scriptures through the lens of your imagination.

SPIRITUAL PRACTICES

Simple lifestyle: Live within a budget without debt wherever possible.

Choose a career based on vocation: Begin with the end in view—what will give you the most pleasure and fulfilment?

Get involved in volunteer community work: What is missing in your community that you can offer (for example, tutoring, community gardening, graffiti cleanup, or recycling litter)?

Social advocacy: Share your ideas and insights with your elected leaders and clergypersons.

Treat all people with kindness and respect: Each interaction is an occasion to test or grow in your spirituality.

FURTHER READING

Nolan, Albert. *Jesus Before Christianity*. Maryknoll, NY: Orbis Books, 1992.

Norris, Kathleen. *Acedia and Me: A Marriage, Monks, and a Writer's Life*. New York: Riverhead Books, 2008.

Wallis, Jim. *The Great Awakening: 7 Ways to Change the World: Reviving Faith and Politics*. New York: HarperCollins, 2008.

Wicks, Robert. *Everyday Simplicity: A Practical Guide to Spiritual Growth*. Notre Dame, IN: Sorin Books, 2000.

7

Sexuality

It's Not Just about SEX!

(Frigidity/Promiscuity)

THE STORY IS TOLD of an elderly pastor who had been at the same church for many years. He and his wife had grown to love the community. One night, as he struggled to prepare his Sunday sermon, he asked his wife for ideas she might have on possible topics. She offered nothing new, so he said, "Then I think I will preach on horseback riding." "Horseback riding?" she retorted, "Why in God's name would you want to preach on horseback riding?" "Because I have preached to this community on every other conceivable topic. I need to talk about something new." "Well, if you're going to preach on that theme, then I am going to stay in the car," she replied, "I don't want to be embarrassed by your lack of knowledge on the topic." As they drove to the church, the pastor tried to change his wife's mind, but she remained firm. During the service, as the pastor stood to deliver the sermon, he was suddenly inspired to deliver a "hellfire and brimstone" talk on sex. It seemed to go well. As the parishioners filed out of the church after the service, a couple of them wandered over to the wife, praising her husband's sermon. She grumbled, "Oh, what does he know about that topic? The first time, he didn't know how to do it, so he fled in fear; the second time he tried it, he fell off; the third and final time, he tried it at a family picnic and my father had to help him!"

The topic of sex and sexuality tends to bring out the best and the worst in people. We talk a lot about sex, and we frequently joke about it, often in colorful ways. But let's face it: we're nervous about it. Much needless guilt and shame is built up around it. Why? We are ashamed of our naked humanness, our earthiness, our wildness. We know, at some intuitive level, that sexuality is the experience of oneself and the expression of oneself. It is rightfully something very personal. Sociologically, sexuality embraces the anthropological, cultural, political, and legal aspects of being human. Biologically, this topic deals with the physiological, psychological, and genital interactions within and between persons. Philosophically, sexuality is viewed from moral, ethical, theological, and religious perspectives.

The word sex comes from the Latin word sexus, meaning to "cut" or "separate." To illustrate this, Plato offers this story of creation: The gods, having decided to create a being similar to themselves, fashioned a large human creature with the features of a man on one side and a woman on the other. As the creature matured, the gods observed that it grew in power. This could not be tolerated, so taking a large sword, they cut the creature in two, thus halving its power. Since then, these two resultant creatures pursue each other in search of reconnection and wholeness.

When faced with the inviting subject of sex, most believers—especially the young—often begin with the simplistic question, "How far can I go?" thus reducing human sexuality to genital activity. Genital activity, ideally, is an expression of something much deeper than physical attraction. The union of bodies is a potent symbolic expression of the union between two hearts, two minds, two souls. This heartfelt and passionate concentration of energy is mediated through the body. Since many of us will find ourselves in situations, whether through choice or circumstance, where genital activity is not available or not desired, how is it possible to find an appropriate expression? Male and female sexualities differ significantly from each other. This difference governs how we relate, how we see the world, and how we prioritize our values. We need both viewpoints to become more engaged with a broader understanding and sense of human sexuality. This God-given dimension of our being is the passion for life itself. This is why sexuality cannot and must not be limited only to one method or means of expression. Sexuality flows through our very being in all that we do, all that we experience (Rolheiser, *Holy Longing*, 192–212). This energy is meant to be creatively and uniquely expressed in the way we live. For some, this may mean gardening, others, reading or writing, while others may express their sexuality through sports or recreation, arts and crafts, or cooking, dancing, music, or even prayer! How do you most enjoy the pleasure of expressing yourself, enjoying the delight of being human? Your answer will indicate the way you uniquely share in the delight of the Creator.

Sexuality, as seen from a spiritual point of view, is a passion or enthusiasm for life, expressed from the depths of our souls. It is the drive toward "other," toward right relationship. This is why any violation of this sacred energy, such as molestation, incest, or rape, is so devastating for the individual. Sexuality and spirituality are two sides of the same coin. Spirituality is about "innerness," while sexuality is focused on "outerness." Both are expressions of yearning for the Divine. When we touch one side, we automatically awaken the other aspect of our humanity. Spirituality and sexuality meet in the human body (Rohr, "Pure Passion"). This is why there is no more effective way to destroy our faith than to destroy the integrity of the body. Judith Plaskow, author of *Standing Again at Sinai*, says, "When we touch the place in our lives where spirituality and sexuality come together, we touch our wholeness and the fullness of our power, and at the same time, our connection with a power larger than ourselves" (197).

A vibrant spirituality must include a healthy approach to our own sexuality. Sex is much broader than genitality, and certainly doesn't have to include genital activity to be vibrant or alive. Sexuality is primarily symbolic energy—in other words, there's more here than meets the eye. So, what is this "more"? The field of depth psychology has provided some language for this area.

A quick word here about depth psychology before we proceed: perhaps an image will be helpful. When at the ocean, people are drawn to different aspects: some simply enjoy the view, some like to wade in, others like to explore in boats, while some few like to dive the depths. Depth psychology "dives the depths" of the human psyche to discover the richness, the power, the sources of life's energies.

Back to the exploration of that symbolic energy we call "sexuality." It demands some effort to understand it and to embrace it in a healthy way. Depth psychology has named this energy *archetypal*. An archetype is a kind of a template for reading reality through metaphors or images. It is a constellation of certain energies and feelings around a figure or image, real or mythical. This template is to the soul what the five senses are to the body. Our senses help us connect with the depths of our individual soul and its myriad forms of energy. In any culture, sexual archetypes will settle upon a particular type of person who embodies a certain energy. We see this, for example, in the world of pop culture that holds up this communal identification for us in such classic characters/types as John Wayne (hero), Marilyn Monroe (goddess), Bruce Willis (warrior), Madonna (temptress), Elvis Presley (rebel). At an individual level, these archetypes will be at play in our own attractions, repulsions, relationships, and fascinations. Falling in love with someone who will "complete us" or "wake us up" to our full potential, or "fulfill all our dreams," is a result of this phenomenon—as is its opposite, a visceral negative response to another person. There are countless numbers of archetypes in the human soul (for example, mother, father, lover, warrior, victim, playboy, and so on.). These are carried for us in numerous stories, movies, images, as well as in the pantheon of the Greek/Roman gods/goddesses. What archetypes have presented themselves to you through dreams, fantasies, repulsions, secret attractions, or repetitive behavior?

Archetypes survive through cultures, generations, and history. They simply change faces and situations. This is not about you and me, per se, but about human beings in general. Understanding this dynamic better can liberate us from unnecessary guilt and shame and help us face the real issues in our lives. There is a true but almost unbelievable story about a woman who had begun therapy ostensibly over the problems she was having in her marriage. As the therapy unfolded, her therapist discovered she had been married five times. He asked, "Do you see the pattern of these relationships? Do you understand what is really happening in your life?" "No," she replied. After further prodding and questioning did not work, the therapist finally said directly, "You have had one marriage repeated five times. Even though each of these men has had a different career and come from different backgrounds, they are all alcoholics." She was incredulous! She never "saw" that truth. Then the real work began. Her interior life was inviting her to deal with the archetype of the alcoholic, which had been with her since her childhood with an alcoholic father.

The temptation for many of us, in the face of our sexuality, is to close down, freeze up, or naïvely accept everything as helpful or good for us. This is the old tension between frigidity and promiscuity. Neither choice is free! Neither is the way to emotional health and well-being. Virtue is always found in the middle! Themes such as femininity, masculinity, possession, dominance, submission, affirmation, belonging, vulnerability, trust, and nurturance weave in and out of our relationships. This sexual energy is an invitation to step into the mystery of being human—a sacred journey involving choices that can unravel us (divisive) or pull us together (unitive). Whatever the fascination, it is an invitation to reflect upon the mystery of our own humanity. So our sexual fantasies prompt us to ask ourselves, what's really happening here? What is the meaning of this attraction or repulsion? What am I looking for—is it excitement, connection, reward, touch, release of tension, healing, intimacy, affirmation? Lustful fantasies can and do spring from a whole range of inner needs and desires. We can observe and experience these feelings, listening to them without judgment or acting out behaviors. Beware of giving in to toxic shame or neurotic guilt!

An old Latin proverb states, "The corruption of the best is the worst." Never is this more apparent or possible than in the area of human sexuality. To live a compartmentalized sexuality is to link ourselves to dysfunctional attitudes and behaviors, while an integrated sexuality leads us to compassion and wholeness. The intimacy and integrity of human relationships, no matter the sexual orientation, is to be respected. This means that the imperatives of mutuality, fidelity, exclusivity, and life-giving love remain the same. Spiritual writer C. S. Lewis once said, "God is wild, you know!" This wildness is manifested throughout creation. It is our task, following the Creator's example, to integrate this wildness of ours into the larger picture of our lives. This is the work of human integrity and wholeness.

Sexuality is the energy for relationships, the endless fascination with the other, the yearning for communion with another person that is expressed in a plethora of ways. It is, as Franciscan priest Richard Rohr says, "the Gateway to the Temple but not the Temple itself." This passion is experienced at different levels of our humanity. It is the yearning for union, wholeness, creativity—for getting inside the mystery of who we are. This is sacred fire! Some people try to repress this energy into their heads, others into their genitals. Neither are free (Rohr, "Pure Passion"). Viewing or reading pornography, for example, can be depressive because it overstimulates the senses by tapping into the "grandiosity" center of our ego. John of the Cross insightfully said, "When the spirit is stimulated, it flows into the senses." This energy must be expressed somewhere, somehow. We can only hope it will be expressed in a life-giving way. Perhaps this is why so many celibates are artists and musicians. Most beautifully, within a committed love partnership, this sacred fire is meant to be expressed in a mutually enriching genital relationship that celebrates the ultimate intimacy of giving oneself totally to another. It is a celebration of closeness and intensity that can be experienced as unitive for many.

To live the symbolic life consciously is to live the spiritual life maturely. This means to live on the right level with the right expressions. Living only at the most superficial or literal level is the bane of the spiritual life. A symbol means much more than its actual physical representation. Symbols carry great weight of meaning and purpose. The practice of relating to objects, ideas, feelings, or to others solely on a literal level is called idolatry, always a danger in the spiritual life. This is why we approach this field of sexuality with humility and reverence, seeking right relationships at all levels of our humanity. This is our responsibility, our transformative life's work. The spiritual life is not about comfort, it is about transformation. Judith Plaskow again, "If sexuality is one dimension of our ability to live passionately in the world, then in cutting off our sexual feelings, we diminish our overall power to feel, know, and value deeply" (187). How, then, do you express your sexual yearnings, your desires? How do you respond to the passion that has been given to you as a co-creator with God?

In John 10:10, we are encouraged by Jesus' words to his disciples: "I came that they may have life, and have it abundantly." Jesus' embodiment is the Divine Affirmation of our humanity in its fullness. This includes our sexuality, our energy for creativity, and our relationships. How might we live out this fullness? I believe we can do this by living a contemplative life with a respectful approach to that which is "other"; to a life of intimacy on four levels.

1. *Contemplative friendship:* form relationships with soul friends, fellow searchers, prayer partners, "playmates"
2. *Contemplative expression:* participate in artwork, music, gardening, dance, writing, poetry
3. *Contemplative prayer:* focus on a single object, breath, image or word, meditation, journaling
4. *Contemplative union:* Respectfully reverencing all of life, reclaiming projections (respectfully expressing one's feelings), honoring your body and its limitations (massages, slow eating, the enjoyment of sensual delights), mutually enriching genital relationship within a committed partnership

QUESTIONS

Do you have healthy vibrant relationships with people other than your committed partner or immediate family?

Do you have relationships that carry an appropriate measure of both intimacy and vulnerability?

Do you see yourself as a healthy, passionate person with a zest for life as witnessed by your way of living?

PRAYER FORMS

Focusing prayer. A guided prayer practice that puts the emphasis on our feelings in our bodies. It asks us to listen to our body knowledge rather than simply our intellectual perceptions.

Prayer of imagination: Seeks the truth of the heart rather than intellectual truth. This form of prayer, inspired by Ignatius of Loyola, works well in conjunction with the Scriptures.

Embodied prayer: Conscious physical expression of our interior disposition (for example, uplifted hands, kneeling, movement, sitting in a comfortable chair, bowing low before an icon). For some, a symbolic gesture like opening a door is a powerful expression of openness to the other.

SPIRITUAL PRACTICES

Artwork/craftwork: Exercises and directs the inner power of creative expression.

Yoga: A generic term for the physical, mental, and spiritual practices that originated in ancient India through Hinduism. These practices seek a way of inner peace.

Vibrant relationships with people of both genders: Intimacy assists us in our quest for wholeness.

Genital activity within a committed relationship: A physical union that can remind us of our intimacy with the Creator.

Respect the unique "otherness" of people: What attracts you or repels you about this person?

FURTHER READING

Cornell, Ann Weiser. *The Power of Focusing: A Practical Guide to Emotional Self-Healing*. Oakland, CA: New Harbinger Publications, 1996.

Ferder, Fran, and John Heagle. *Your Sexual Self: Pathway to Authentic Intimacy*. Notre Dame, IN: Ave Maria Press, 1992.

Whitehead, James, and Evelyn Whitehead. *Wisdom of the Body: Making Sense of Our Sexuality*. New York: Crossroad, 2001.

8

Silence
Sh-hhhhhhhh

(Violence/Meaninglessness)

WE LIVE IN A WORLD OF NOISE. External noises of traffic, talk radio, music, television, conversation, machines, are matched by the inner disquiet of worries, anxieties, and unresolved past memories or conversations. Incessant noise violates the natural inborn sensitivity of the human soul. When the soul is neglected, we can feel as though we have lost meaning in our lives. This can sometimes lead us into addictions, obsessive compulsions, and even violence. French philosopher, Blaise Pascal once declared, "All human evil comes from a single cause, man's [sic] inability to sit still in a room." So much violence happens because so few people are willing to take time to be in silence.

Our world is violent for many reasons, but at the heart of the problem is the fact that we have forgotten how to be silent, how to turn off the noise or mute its effects in our lives. As Richard Rohr says, the fate of the soul is the fate of the social order. In looking at U.S. society, we can't help but wonder about the state of our cultural soul, when we live in such a violent culture with a thin veneer of entertainment to distract us. In some quarters of society, violence has become an acceptable form of entertainment. Silence helps to reconnect us with our creative self and re-centers us in our authentic nature. Being silent is a means of attending to the needs of the soul. It puts us in touch with our deepest desires.

Many years ago, when I was feeling overworked and stressed from my parochial obligations, I went to visit family members. As I was driving in a small car during afternoon rush hour, I found myself stopped at a traffic light behind an old pickup truck containing two young men. Behind me was a long line of vehicles waiting for the light to change. When the light turned green, the truck moved forward a few feet into the intersection and then stopped for no apparent reason. I looked into my rearview mirror and noticed that all the vehicles behind me were moving around me. The two young men were laughing and pointing in my direction. For whatever reason, I thought they were making fun of my predicament, so I foolishly made an obscene gesture at them, which caused an immediate reaction by the passenger. He came out from the truck and proceeded to kick in my front passenger door. I realized the dangerous predicament I was in, so I moved into the next lane without saying or doing anything else that would cause a further escalation of violence. I drove to my brother's house without further incident, but I was filled with a stew of dark emotions: fear, sadness, confusion, shame, and guilt. As I pondered my actions and reactions, I felt blocked from any real self-understanding of what had just happened. Since this behavior was so out of character for me, I didn't know what to do. I was stunned and ashamed of myself. Finally, I did the only thing I knew would work. I listened in silence. As I remained silent, some bits of insight slowly bubbled to the surface. I had recently made a public vow of nonviolence, and here I was, acting in a quite violent public manner—a real disparity between word and action! I then brought this disparity to prayer and sensed that God was saying, "You asked to become a man of nonviolence; I am showing you how violent you are in your attitudes." This was a humbling response indeed, but just what I needed to further my own growth.

Silence was the key in resolving this dilemma. After a family altercation, a rash judgment, a loss of focus at work, even an overwhelming reaction or attraction to someone, or if you are simply feeling "blue" or depressed, it might be most helpful to take some quiet time to reconnect with your core self. Just sit in silence and wait for the interior conversation to begin. Let go of expectations and see where the presence of the Spirit leads you. Silence helps us not to over-identify with our thoughts, feelings, or experiences. It can offer us a greater illumination and compassion in facing the humbling truth about ourselves.

In 1 Kings 19:9–13, we read the story of the prophet Elijah's encounter with God. Elijah is being pursued by enemies who want to put him to the sword. He is guided to a cave on Mt. Horeb where he is told to wait for the coming of the Lord. In succession, he experiences a strong wind, an earthquake, and a fire, but notes that the Lord was not in any of them. Then he heard "a sound of sheer silence," which he recognized as the presence of the Lord. Silence is the first language of God. When we practice this language often, it is likely that we will recognize the presence of the Lord more clearly, as Elijah did, in the daily activities of our lives. This Presence does not announce itself noisily, but rather, permeates our lives as a quiet force of energy.

Out of silence comes a greater clarity or groundedness. Spiritual writer Esther de Waal speaks of her experience, "Unless I am silent I shall not hear God, and until I hear God I shall not come to know God. Silence asks me to watch and wait and listen....If I have any respect for God I shall try to find a time, however short, for silence" (*Seeking God*, 146). Many people who have made a silent retreat speak of seeing things more clearly or their lives slowing down so that the essential aspects are more deeply appreciated. This can lead to creative insights or projects, as well as a resurgence of energy flowing from the deep wellsprings of the human soul.

Silence leads us to reconnect with the natural rhythm of holding on and letting go, like the back-and-forth motion of the ocean's waves. It might be that this natural rhythm can help us in one of the more difficult tasks that face us as human beings—that of forgiveness. Forgiveness is a regular, sustained practice of living in this natural rhythm of creation. At its core, forgiveness is choosing to let go of the past in order to live in the present. Letting go of blame and accepting reality as it is makes for a peaceful state of being and right relationship.

Silence is like breathing in and out, reminding us that nothing lasts forever. We only have this moment for a fleeting second and then it is gone. In the Jewish faith, this truth is expressed most convincingly. There is no one Hebrew word for God, since God cannot be named, only described.

One of these descriptive words for the Creator is *Yahweh*. I understand that this is the only Hebrew word where the speaker's tongue does not touch the palate in the recitation of the word. As one speaks this two-syllable word slowly, *Yah-weh*, it sounds like a single breath-in-and-out. The Jews believe that the first word and the last word that every human being speaks is the "name" of God, Yahweh, the only lasting Presence in creation. What a potent reminder to us of what is fundamental and central to our human be-ingness.

Silence often leads to some form of prayer. I imagine Jesus communing with Abba in the silent interiority of his heart when he went off to pray in solitude. He made these excursions before making any major decisions in his life. Silence reminds us that some things are worth waiting for, without rushing to a conclusion too soon.

Finally, and most practically, in a busy life, silence serves as a contemplative pause between the endless active scenarios that necessarily fill our lives. Silence slows us down long enough to "see" and understand the meaning and significance of the events of our lives. Whether it is a momentary pause in the day, such as taking a break from our cell phone or computer, or a quiet sit in the park, silence can serve to offer perspective to some of the most troubling aspects of our lives. Carl Jung once said that we rarely solve our problems—rather we tend to outgrow them. Because of our need to protect our ego, and appear in control, we will often find that the vast majority of our thoughts tend to be negative and repetitive. We can use silence as a technique to interrupt this flow of negativity, and to move into another track of thought that is more invigorating and life-giving. What happens to you when you are silent before life's great mysteries: love, joy, suffering, pain, loss?

QUESTIONS

What forms of distraction do you use to avoid facing inner pain?

What form of prayer sustains you in dark times of turmoil?

How do you let go of your attachments to past mistakes or failures?

PRAYER FORMS

Centering prayer: An interior focus on one word, image, or symbol that frees the heart to be present to God in a contemplative manner.

Healing of memories: Entering the scene of a past painful memory and reexperiencing it in the imagined presence of Christ, releasing the attachment to the pain.

Breathing: Focus on the inhalation and exhalation of each breath.

SPIRITUAL PRACTICES

Establishment of a dedicated time/place in your home for regular prayer/silence: A particular chair, room, or place where you will not be disturbed. Taking solitary walks without an iPod or other electronic devices.

Real presence: Do one thing at a time.

Labyrinth: In the Middle Ages, Christians would often lay an intricate, symbolic pattern in the floor of a church, to be walked by pilgrims. This unicursal path to a designated center and its return is often seen as a journey or pilgrimage that an individual or a community can follow on a floor or earth.

Silent retreat: Varying lengths from hours to days or weeks.

FURTHER READING

Blythe, Teresa A. *50 Ways to Pray: Practices from Many Traditions and Times.* Nashville: Abingdon Press, 2006.

Funk, Mary Margaret. *Thoughts Matter: The Practice of the Spiritual Life.* New York: Continuum, 1998.

K., Herb. *Twelve Steps to Spiritual Awakening: Enlightenment for Everyone.* Torrance, CA: Capizon Publishing, 2010.

Rohr, Richard. *Everything Belongs: The Gift of Contemplative Prayer.* New York: Crossroad, 2003.

9

Simplification
Drop Your Bundle

(Materialism/Consumerism)

WHEN WE FEEL INADEQUATE or incomplete, we often seek to fill the void with something tangible: a toy, a dress, a car, food, a person, or a title. There is nothing wrong or evil about these choices. It's just that they do not really fill the emptiness or satiate the hunger for affirmation or wholeness. This misplacement or misunderstanding of our deep hunger for completion can be exacerbated to the point where it can manifest itself in obesity, hoarding, materialism, addictions, and compulsions of all sorts. The proper response to this inner yearning is not to reach for more, but rather, to stand in the gap and accept the unacceptable truth: I am incomplete. Nothing can completely satisfy me—no person, object, or experience—only the Creator. As Augustine said so eloquently, "Our hearts are restless until they rest in thee, O Lord."

Despite all the weaknesses in my life, the gaps, the needs, the missing bits, I am, indeed, enough; I have enough; this moment is enough. Accepting reality as it is sounds so simple, but simple things are often the most difficult things to do. This is the great wisdom of the saints and the mystics. To live in this moment, with this attitude, is what creates happiness, joy, and fulfillment. This is why each religious tradition honors the simple life. Wisdom, the great saints tell us, is found in simplicity. Living with less offers us the opportunity to see more clearly into the essence and beauty of life. The more we carry through life—more worries, possessions, projects, ambitions, prejudices, and so on, the harder it is to experience this beauty.

It helps to unpack this excess baggage by taking a deeper look at the underpinnings of this attitude—this inability to accept our limitations. As I see it, there are four layers that contribute to this misdirection of our interior life that leads to an unhealthy relationship to possessions. Each layer leads to the next.

1. Free-floating thoughts whose validity is unquestioned
2. Attitudes that have become calcified without reflective input
3. Behavior that is an automatic or unthinking response to outward stimuli
4. Possessions accrued as a primary source of comfort and security

This is the antithesis of faith. If I start with the premise that "I must be comfortable at all costs" then this becomes the idolatrous focus of my life. Everything and everyone must bow down before this altar. It follows, then, that this attitude will influence the way that I achieve comfort. Each of us will choose a different means of creating a comfortable situation for ourselves. The possessions are symbolic expressions of this belief system. Again, there is nothing inherently wrong with this perspective, to a point. It just does not go far enough. Faith is about facing reality as it is. What is required is an attitude of searching for the Divine in each situation, with the express hope and intention of active engagement.

Fulfillment comes not from having more possessions but from right relationship to all that is. Try this some time when you are shopping, especially for a big-ticket item. Ask yourself: what does this item represent to me? Greater prestige? More influence? Better appearance? Sometimes it helps just to go window-shopping and notice the particular products or services that attract you, without buying them. Avoiding the natural inclination to give into instant gratification opens up all sorts of possibilities. Sit with the tension, the yearning. This practice can better assist you in understanding your own particular cravings. Look at the cravings and reflect on what they mean to you. I know one woman who just cannot buy enough purses; for another, it's shoes. Some men collect tools of all sorts, for others it's sports memorabilia. Hoarding has become a new art. The human soul expresses itself in a symbolic, metaphoric fashion. To learn the language and to make conscious choices is to live the moral life, the liberated life of the Spirit. This is where the regular practice of discernment among different "goods" fits into a vibrant spirituality.

Less is better than more in the spiritual life. A spirituality of subtraction assists us in seeing more clearly through the created objects to the Creator. One Lent, Bishop Robert Morneau decided to put this concept into practice by committing himself to give away something every day. One day he gave away a sweater to someone in need. Another day he smiled at a stranger, and the following day, he gave the gift of his time to someone who needed a listening ear and heart. As this daily conscious practice unfolded, he discovered the ancient circular wisdom of giving away possessions. We really don't possess anything or anyone. All is given as gift to be shared with others at the opportune time.

For some tribes within the Native American tradition there is a ritual called the "giving away ceremony," similar to potlatch, wherein the participants anonymously give away something they no longer need, recognizing that someone else could use the item. This ceremony comes from a culture that believes that to die with no possessions is a sign of a happy and good life. It means that you have had many friends and family members with whom to share your possessions. Contrast this with the unspoken mantra of the dominant American culture, "The one who dies with the most toys wins!" Faith is living without attachments, and at the same time being connected to everything.

Perhaps it comes with age or wisdom, but the older I get, the less I need and the happier I am. When I was younger, I used to carry all sorts of stuff that I thought I needed or would eventually need or someone else would ask me for. Now that I am more settled, I realize that I was carrying what I thought I "should" carry in life. Faith is carrying our own stuff in partnership with God; no more, no less. As we grow in faith, we come to realize that God asks us to carry very little on our journey. But what we carry is priceless.

Materialism and consumerism are dangerous, in that these attitudes can create a false sense of independence and self-absorption. Our human needs remind us of our interconnectedness and real need to share with others. Life is not about collecting more—it is about sharing more. The Chinese philosopher Lao Tzu puts it succinctly, "To know that you have enough is to be rich."

In Matthew 4:1–11, Jesus faced three temptations that revolved around the use of power, prestige, and possessions. In essence, these are temptations to settle for less than the fullness of one's humanity. Jesus' courageous response to each of these invitations is a model for humans who struggle with similar temptations to settle for a life without depth of meaning, or care for others. These temptations remind us to be wary of greed in all its many disguises. How much of your time is spent cleaning, protecting, storing, and multiplying your possessions, expanding your influence, and polishing your reputation? To live from the center of one's life is the task of every human being; otherwise we are constantly reacting to everything that comes our way.

One of the cultural challenges that believers face in Western civilization is, "How do I live an interdependent life in a fast paced society that proclaims loudly: 'Become independent!'?" One way to approach this dilemma is to change your mindset. You do not have to own everything that is "necessary" for a self-sustaining environment. The early Christian communities shared everything in common (Acts 2:44–45) as another means of creating life-sustaining support networks and reminding one another that together they had enough. This insight can be lived out in family structures, communities, and local neighborhoods. My cousin, Julie Ann, told me once that if she cannot remember each of her pairs of shoes or dresses, then it is time to give some away. And so she does. To live within our means is a practiced choice that can change our lives. Happiness is something that comes not from external circumstances or possessions, but from an inner attitude of contentment and gratitude.

QUESTIONS

For what do you want to be remembered?

Can you name everything you own? If not, what needs to go?

What can you let go of, so that your journey is more enjoyable?

How can you simplify your life?

PRAYER FORMS

Short repetitive prayers: Our Father; Lord, have mercy; Thank you; Help me; Guide me.

Spontaneous prayer. Speak honestly and humbly from your heart.

SPIRITUAL PRACTICES

Observe self-talk: Negativity and self-deprecation serve only to de-energize you. Let them go and change your self-talk.

Regularly clean out wardrobe closets, garage, attic, storage rooms: Share with those in need.

Tithe a portion of your income to charity: Regular sharing of your income connects you with a larger community and purpose.

Write your own eulogy: How do you want to be remembered?

Each week, give something away: A smile to a stranger, a jacket you no longer need, your attentive time listening to someone in pain.

Reduce-reuse-recycle: What kind of environment do you want to pass on to the next generation?

FURTHER READING

The Earth Works Group. *50 Simple Things You Can Do to Save the Earth*. Berkeley, CA: Earthworks Press, 1989.

Hollis, James. *What Matters Most: Living a More Considered Life*. New York: Gotham Books, 2009.

Whitehead, Evelyn E., and James D. Whitehead. *Seasons of Strength: New Visions of Adult Christian Maturing*. Winona, MN: St. Mary's Press, 1995.

10

Symbolic Life
Everything Ain't What It Seems

(Literalism/Fundamentalism)

ALL OF LIFE HAS MEANING. To live life only at a literal level is to miss
the full vitality of reality. Let me explain. Hidden in the details of every life
is the magnificent wonder of many levels of meaning and potential.
Depending upon the context of my life, I can view objects and events
through a number of different lenses—for example, scientific, political,
relational, or economic. From the perspective of the soul, to view my life
imaginally means to see with new eyes, to experience with a new heart.
This is the language of the Sacred Scriptures, the mystic tradition, and the
world of symbolic expression.

I've said it before, but it bears repeating: literalism is the bane of religion and has caused untold human suffering. Mythologist Joseph Campbell
puts it this way, "Every religion is true one way or another. It is true when
understood metaphorically. But when it gets stuck in its own metaphors,
interpreting them as facts, then you are in trouble" (*The Power of Myth*,
67). This is true whether we are speaking about the Scriptures, images,
or the practices of our religion. Healthy religion, when practiced with
awareness, is a humble acknowledgment of the Mystery of the Other
through the avenue of imagination, the birthplace of faith. It is no surprise, therefore, that many different religions or ways have emerged of
celebrating and honoring this Mystery. We variously use the names God,

Yahweh, Allah, or other descriptors in an attempt to address the Divine Being. None of these, of course, literally "name" the Divine.

The language of the soul is always metaphorical or symbolic. Consequently, most traditional religions, when respectfully describing and honoring this Sacred Reality, must resort to the use of symbols and metaphors. A symbol is much more than a literal sign. A symbol points beyond itself, holding together in its essence a multiplicity of meanings that touch each individual uniquely. In other words, a symbol is what it is, and much more.

Let me tell you the story of a farmer who understood this power of symbol very well. Every evening as he drove back to his house, after the day's work, the farmer would ponder all the problems and worries that he had in managing the farm—paying the mortgage, crop failure, and the endless unfinished tasks. In his imagination, he put all these anxieties into his old hat. Just before getting out of his truck, he took off his hat and gently placed it on the seat. Conscious that in this way he could leave all his concerns right there, he entered his house with a positive spirit, ready to be present to his family. The next morning, he would once again put on his hat and all that it symbolized.

Here are a couple of more familiar examples: think of a $50 bill (literally a slip of printed paper), or the flag (literally a piece of cloth with a specified design). Both simple objects, but carrying tremendous power and meaning beyond their obvious attributes and makeup. A sign, on the other hand, is what it is and no more—a messenger of sorts (think of a stop sign). British writer Margot Asquith once said, "Symbols are the imaginative signposts of life." We are not to worship the signposts; rather, we are to follow their guidance. Many religious believers confuse signs and symbols, often pitting "scientific" truth over and against imaginal reality. Both are true from their own viewpoints. Symbols can be used for good (as in drawing people together) or for ill (as in destruction and divisiveness), as has been seen through the centuries. Religious wars usually occur when traditional beliefs, symbols, and practices are subjected to compartmentalization and literal application.

The rise of fundamentalism in society should be no surprise to us. It is an ideology that seeks to simplistically reduce everything down to an easy explanation. This attitude is not limited to religion per se; it can be found in a number of fields of human endeavor, including science, politics, and sports. It is a universal human temptation, not just a religious struggle. It is so easy to find security and identity in "black and white" truths. Recognizing and accepting the complexity of life with its paradoxical challenges is the first step to maturity. This is especially true when we are dealing with the Sacred. Anything can be turned into an idol, deified or given the place of highest importance: ideas, feelings, images, words, symbols, possessions, titles, and so on.

The mythic imagination and the scientific mind are not meant to be oppositional. On the contrary, when these two aspects of our humanity are working properly, they are not combative, but mutually supportive. Each viewpoint offers us a way of engaging the mysteries of reality that will assist us in our search for meaning. If, however, we confuse their different roles, then we will misinterpret their discoveries and meanings.

Living the symbolic life is a means, not an end. It strengthens and fortifies the interior life in preparation for the external struggles we all have. Good religion leads and guides the believer to an encounter with the Holy. For behind the literal symbol or the Sacred Scripture is the great myth or story into which each one of us is invited to enter. For example, in broad terms, the Hindu story is about renewal and rebirth; the Buddhist philosophy is that suffering is self-made and therefore can be alleviated with the right discipline; the Jewish story seeks right relationships with God, others and the world; Christianity proclaims the equality, blessedness, and love of all people; and Islam is focused on submission to Allah and the discipline of caring for the tradition and its teachings (Chittister, *Welcome to the Wisdom of the World*, 167–86). It is not enough to understand intellectually the teachings of these and other religions. We must *experience* the Mystery proclaimed. This is the mystical element of all religions—knowing God rather than knowing *about* God. Perhaps the recent surge of interest in the field of spirituality is, at its core, driven by a desire to experience God personally and directly, and not through a mediator such as a clergyperson or sacred book. How do you enter the story of your religion, or a particular symbol, so that it has personal significance for you? Without personal engagement, we are left with a musical score but no melody or sound.

Healthy religion evolves over time to express its core beliefs in ever new and fresh ways. When religion fails to do this well, it becomes desiccated, brittle, and harsh in its judgments of others. In Deuteronomy 5:11, we read, "You shall not invoke the name of the LORD, your God, in vain" (NABRE). Scripture scholars tell us that this passage is addressed to this very topic of respecting the words and images we use to describe God and the sacred life so that it does not become brittle and lifeless. The commandment is not primarily about avoiding cursing and swearing; rather, these words are directed toward those of us who would attempt to definitively ascribe particular words, descriptions, images, and signs to God. God cannot be limited to any one image, title, or sign. The American novelist Joyce Carol Oates once remarked, "Homo sapiens is the species that invents symbols in which to invest passion, and authority, then forgets symbols are inventions." So, at our best, we aim to respectfully craft a system of words, images, and symbols to describe God and our relationship with this Divine Presence, knowing that they will change over time.

This is where *consciously* living a symbolic life can be profoundly helpful in enlivening our faith and spirituality, for a liberating spirituality is continually expansive and transformative. We choose the meaning and significance of an event, circumstance, or object. This is what works to bring out the depth of our interior life and can help us discover our own interior bliss and joy. For example, you can go to work focused on "earning a living," or you can deepen this truth by imagining yourself participating in the building up of the community. You could place the emphasis on making sure your kids get to school on time each morning, or you could see this regular event as an opportunity to teach your children the discipline of honoring time and commitment to a higher goal.

What, then, are the ways available to us to live the symbolic life consciously and with discipline? Traditionally this has been through participating in communal gatherings, rituals, and practices. For example, the ancient Greeks named and celebrated the vagaries of humanity by creating a pantheon of gods and goddesses. Their great myths were a form of sacred psychology, inviting religious practitioners to learn from the struggles of these gods. Hindus live symbolically by attaching themselves to a specific god, making daily offerings of food and prayers to sustain the internal life. Catholics and Orthodox Christians live out a sacramental life as a way of reminding themselves that God is present in all of reality, expressing God's self through the ordinary events and circumstances of life (birth, relationships, meals, marriage, death).

In this connection, there is a wonderful story told about a missionary priest sent to an African tribe that had never heard about Christianity. The bishop had told the priest to go and baptize these "pagans." After two years, the bishop inquired as to how many people he had baptized. "None," said the priest. "Well what have you been doing all this time?" the bishop asked. "I've been talking to them about God's love. They are listening well," replied the priest. "Very well, continue on then, but don't forget we want to begin baptisms soon," said the bishop. The priest continued his labors among the people with great determination. One year later, the bishop inquired again about the priest's progress. When he was told that there were still no baptisms or other sacraments administered by the priest, he was nonplussed. He decided to visit the mission to oversee the situation himself. When he arrived, the bishop asked for an interpreter so he could speak to the whole community. He began by speaking about God's love and the people all smiled and nodded in agreement, acknowledging their acceptance and understanding. He then continued: "God shows his love for us in seven ways called sacraments." The people began to murmur in confusion. Finally the elder of the community stood and faced the bishop and said through the interpreter: "Bishop, only seven ways??? We experience God through creation, the rain, the crops, the blessings of friendship and food, and now this good news that God loves us at all times. No, we disagree. God loves us in many ways." The elder then sat down, leaving the bishop to ponder this piece of wisdom alone.

Of course, God is not limited in the ways that Divine Love and Presence are expressed. How do you experience God's presence? How do you respond to this presence? The very things that give energy and liveliness to religions are often missing in contemporary gatherings. The active engagement with creation, imagination, ritual, dreams, story, and artistic expression can enliven and deepen your spirituality. How can you apply this to your own life? In my life, I have reclaimed these missing aspects in various ways. One way that has worked very well for me—which may be surprising—is the reading of novels that engage the unlived (but perfectly legitimate) aspects of my life. For example, stories featuring the successful detective who always solves impossible mysteries, or the super hero who rides into town and brings rough justice, or deeply moving love stories. In this way, I use my imagination and enter the story with "new eyes." Stories of love, suffering, moral dilemmas, and death evoke all sorts of good interior struggles that assist me in my own spiritual and emotional development. What works for you?

QUESTIONS

What are the three most important passions in your life? Would others agree?

What are some important symbols or symbolic expressions in your life?

How do you bring deeper meaning to the ordinary events of your day?

PRAYER FORMS

Seasonal prayer: Praying through the seasons of your life.

Music: Singing, chanting, listening to, or creating music.

Creation: Praying imaginally through different aspects of creation.

SPIRITUAL PRACTICES

Reading good literature: Connecting with the stories and imaginations of other human beings throughout history.

Attending to dreams and active imagination: Actively listening and responding to the ruminations of the interior life.

Shadow work: Welcome and integrate the unacceptable and underexpressed parts of your humanity.

Ritual making: Creating rituals to honor times of transition and to work through emotionally blocked periods.

Artwork: Expressing emotions through color, sound, and/or images.

FURTHER READING

Driver, Tom F. *Liberating Rites: Understanding the Transformative Power of Ritual*. Boulder, CO: Westview Press, 1998.

Johnson, Robert. *Inner Work: Using Dreams and Active Imagination for Personal Growth*. San Francisco: Harper & Row, 1986.

Johnson, Robert, and Jerry Ruhl. *Living Your Unlived Life: Coping with Unrealized Dreams and Fulfilling Your Purpose in the Second Half of Life*. New York: Jeremy P. Tarcher/Penguin, 2007.

Moore, Thomas. *Original Self: Living with Paradox and Originality*. New York: HarperCollins, 2000.

Rohr, Richard. *The Naked Now: Learning to See as the Mystics See*. New York: Crossroad, 2009.

11

Spaciousness
Make Room: Here Comes Everything
(Small-mindedness/Prejudices)

HAVE YOU EVER EXPERIENCED the vastness of the Grand Canyon in Arizona, or Big Sky country in Montana, or the view from atop Mount Whitney, California, on a clear day? If so, like many others, you probably found yourself describing the experience in "spiritual" terms. Contrast this type of experience with being confined to a work cubicle the size of a large closet, or stuck in downtown rush-hour traffic, or the close confines of an MRI tube awaiting a prescribed test. The description of this latter type of experience is generally the polar opposite. Why? We have been created by a spacious God with a depth and breadth that is beyond us and yet within us. We identify ourselves with spaciousness. Narrowness of perception and confined places don't "fit" us as humans.

Scientists have discovered that whether exploring inner space at an atomic level, or outer space at a cosmic level, the message is clear: there is a vastness about creation that presents us with the mysterious reality that much of matter is composed of "empty" space. In truth, the facts are so mind-boggling, so full of wonder, that we are often left scratching our heads in sheer incredulity. Unfortunately, this twenty-first-century scientific imagination is not evenly balanced with a mythic imagination, and so arises a dichotomy or distrust between the two. It seems that some people cannot accept that truth can be both discovered and revealed. These two different approaches do not have to be at odds with each other.

We must observe and respect a developmental understanding of creation and the Creator, or we are left with fundamentalism and/or superstition. There are levels and layers of comprehension and unfolding of one's faith, theology, understanding of the Scriptures, and spirituality. A developmental approach accepts truth in all aspects of reality and from other world religions, recognizing that truth cannot be captured or imprisoned by any one group or religion. An evolving understanding of reading reality accepts that there is truth at each stage. How one reads or tells the story of one's own life as well as the mysteries of life in general, can imprison, limit, liberate, or heal. Maturity necessarily involves seeing the story from an expansive viewpoint, with many different entry points. As Richard Rohr is fond of saying, "How we view anything is how we view everything."

God invites us to see as God sees, expansively and with spaciousness. To move from a small-minded approach to life to a large-minded view is transformational. This involves transcending previous stages of development and growing into our unique humanity (see 1 Cor 13:11–12). God desires human maturity and fulfillment much more than innocence, for we are God's partners in life. We see this truth played out in the archetypal story of Abraham and Isaac (Gen 22:1–18). As the two walked together to the place of sacrifice, the boy Isaac asked his father, "Where is the lamb for a burnt offering?" Abraham replied, "God himself will provide the lamb for a burnt offering" (v. 8). Abraham then proceeded to build an altar at the designated site of the sacrifice. He placed Isaac on top of the wood on the altar, and he reached out with the knife to slaughter his son, but the lord's messenger (angel) intervened with the instructions, "Do not lay your hand on the boy or do anything to him" (v. 12). Abraham followed the directive and was then affirmed for his great faith in God and obedience to God's will.

There are a few different ways to engage this moving story of faith. Depending upon the interpretation, one can discover a horrible image of a petulant God, a story of a religiously disillusioned old man who is willing to kill his only son to satisfy the "Voice," or a story of liberation for all human beings. At the time of the telling of this Scripture, most of the religions in the Middle East practiced some form of child sacrifice as a means to expiate themselves before the gods. Is it possible, we might ask, that Yahweh asked Abraham to go through the long ordeal of waiting for a promised son, only to command him to sacrifice that son on a desert altar so that Abraham could more fully identify with those who have had to sacrifice what is most precious to them? I imagine that God might have used this experience to show Abraham that he did not want child sacrifice. Perhaps God used the look of love and trust of his son to wake Abraham up to this truth. In this equal look of love, Abraham was transformed. God did indeed provide for the sacrifice. It was Abraham's old way of looking at and doing religious things without reflection that was sacrificed. A new era was born, so much so that Abraham is called the Father of Faith in the three major religions whose origins are in the Middle East. This is a good example of growth in religious understanding and practice. In our own time, how many outdated practices and beliefs need to be sacrificed on the altar of our individual or group egos? Almost invariably, God uses the innocent and vulnerable in the world to wake up the powerful to new ways of being human.

I imagine that as Abraham reflected back on this event in which he almost took his son's life, he must have experienced some measure of guilt or regret. What do you think? Guilt and regret often are mixed up in the mind of believers. Many of us forget the difference between the two. Guilt is a legitimate recognition of intentional destructive behavior, whereas regret is an emotional response to events or behaviors that one wishes never occurred or over which, perhaps, we had incomplete control and certainly no intention of malice. The proper response to guilt is remorse and seeking of forgiveness, while the healthy response to regret is a forward-looking resolution that seeks to learn from the experience.

Scripture scholar Walter Brueggemann offers us an insightful way of reading the Scriptures following the canonical layout of the bible:

1. Torah (law and order)—conformist stage that strengthens tribal identity
2. Prophetic literature (prophetic insight)—transformational stage that broadens awareness of global connection

3. Wisdom literature (wisdom of paradox)—mystical stage that leads to awareness of inner divine nature (The Creative Word)

Each category has its own truth and integrity within the right context. One category naturally unfolds into the next. So it is in the canon of the Bible, and so it is meant to be for each of us, as our faith, theology, and spirituality develop and progress. For example, because of his experience of God as Abba, Jesus moved away from the notion of holiness as following a purity code (first stage) to holiness as right relationship with all creation (second stage). Following in the wisdom tradition, Jesus reflected on the human condition and noted that it was love, suffering, and prayer that assisted people in moving forward in their development (third stage) to a mystical connection with the Divine.

Many years ago, my mother made a contemplative retreat and discovered this truth in a personal way. She innocently asked the retreat master, "Do you mean to say that all I have to do in this life is to let God love me as I am and to share that love with others?" "Yes," he said, "All your prayers, works, and struggles are the ground from which this love is to flow." "Well it's all so simple then," she tearfully replied, "I have spent my whole life trying to earn God's love. I like this way better." God is everywhere and desires to be accessible to everyone at all times. We must believe that to live from this space is to see clearly and to delight in the mystery of being divinized creatures. In the face of such great love, surely all fears and prejudices can gradually melt away.

We often cannot accept or trust the next stage of our ongoing development. It's too frightening, so we tend to disparage it, attack it, or deny it. This is why we tend to silence or kill the prophetic voices around us. We will do almost anything to avoid growth, including continuing to live in a self-imposed prison of fear, darkness, and ignorance. Oftentimes this is manifested in various forms of control. The most oft-quoted statement in the Christian Scriptures is "Do not be afraid!" Fear impedes our growth and limits our ability to move forward in our development. This is why the gift and regular practice of discernment between that which enlivens and expands and that which contorts and constricts the human person and condition is a necessary tool for growth and maturity.

Jesus often asked his listeners, "How do you read this?" This was his invitation to them—and to us—to grow up and join the discussion and reflection on the mysteries of life. Trust in and learn from the mystery of your own life and your relationship with God. Life with God is always grace overflowing, boundaries and boxes expanding to include the unknown. God is beyond it all and yet paradoxically within it all at the same time. Henri Nouwen popularized this understanding with his insistence throughout his writings that we are indeed the beloved of God.

This sense of spaciousness and expansion of horizons is experienced by seeking, searching, and delighting in the new and different. It is embodied in the stories of explorers, adventurers, and wanderers of all sorts. How might this expansive approach fit into your life in your relationships, your ideas, your interactions, and your politics?

QUESTIONS

What image of God do you have?

What image of yourself do you have?

How do these images affect your relationship with others?

PRAYER FORMS

Reflecting on moments of surprise, synchronicity, and serendipity: What is the lesson to be learned here?

Contemplation: A simple loving way of being present to what is, through silent observation and restful prayer.

Lectio Divina: A slow contemplative way of praying the Scriptures or other reading material. This method can be used individually or communally. The method involves a four-step process: read, meditate, pray, and contemplate.

Creation: Experiencing the beauty of seeing, touching, smelling, and listening to the sounds of the created world.

Vision quest: A rite of passage in some Native American cultures that provides deep understanding of one's identity and life purpose. Typically, the one-to-four day experience, secluded in nature, provides the opportunity for the individual to experience deep communion with the Creator through the ancient lessons of creation.

SPIRITUAL PRACTICES

Pilgrimage: Journeying to a particular place of significance (religious or secular) as a symbolic means of expressing an internal truth (birthplace, early family home, high school or college reunion, Jerusalem, Rome).

Twelve-step work: A set of guiding principles to help a person in recovery from addictions, compulsions, or other behavioral problems.

Spiritual direction: Meeting with a wise or spiritually mature person who can assist you in your spiritual journey.

Spiritual reading: Regular short daily reading of uplifting material that expands your awareness.

Rekindle wonder and awe in your life: Look at the nighttime sky with "new" eyes.

Write your life story: Make peace with all aspects of your life.

FURTHER READING

Bourgeault, Cynthia. *The Wisdom Way of Knowing: Reclaiming an Ancient Tradition to Awaken the Heart.* San Francisco: Jossey-Bass, 2003.

Cannato, Judy. *Field of Compassion: How the New Cosmology Is Transforming Spiritual Life.* Notre Dame, IN: Sorin Books, 2010.

Casey, Michael. *Sacred Reading: The Ancient Art of Lectio Divina.* Liguori, MO: Liguori Publications, 1997.

Chittister, Joan. *Welcome to the Wisdom of the World and Its Meaning for You: Universal Spiritual Insights Distilled from Five Religious Traditions.* Grand Rapids, MI: Eerdmans, 2007.

Plotkin, Bill. *Soulcraft: Crossing into the Mysteries of Nature and Psyche.* Novato, CA: New World Library, 2003.

12

Stillness
Stop! In the Name of Love!
(Anxiety/Fear)

MANY YEARS AGO, AS PART of a wilderness retreat, I participated in a ropes course, high above the forest floor. One of the participants was an older woman named Elizabeth, who had partnered with a younger woman for this particular exercise. The two of them expertly maneuvered through the first five stages but became stuck on the final stage when Elizabeth froze with fear after looking down to the forest floor, fifty feet below. This last stage involved walking alone across a forty-foot log without holding onto anything stable. The safety line provided did very little to engender confidence, and Elizabeth had walked out only three steps onto the log when she had a panic attack. Despite encouraging words from her partner and guidance from the facilitator, she was stuck and quickly became lost in her own fear. David, the facilitator, then hurried up the tree to stand directly in front of Elizabeth. He told her to look into his eyes and nowhere else. With that, he then invited her to take a deep breath and slide her right foot forward six inches, which she did, trustingly. Then the left foot went forward six inches. With each step, Elizabeth slowly reclaimed her balance and groundedness. She walked all the way to the other side, victorious in reaching her goal.

This story illustrates both a simple way to live, and how to face our fears and anxieties:

- Be still.
- Focus.
- Breathe deeply.
- Move slowly.

Archetypal psychologist James Hillman once said that an illness causes the most suffering before it is named. I have certainly found this to be true in my own life. Over the years, I have developed a simple three-step process to address the illnesses of life. It consists of naming, taming, and claiming the various components of the illness or situation. Naming the real fear or anxiety, for example, is the first step to healing. In this story, Elizabeth is deathly afraid of falling and becoming paralyzed. This fear has become symbolically represented by her emotional paralysis and inability to move forward on the log. She tamed the fear through outside assistance and guidance by focusing on her breath and on the eyes of David. She then claimed her newfound courage by persistently moving forward to her goal, despite the underlying fear. Virtue is hard work. It is never won easily. Perhaps this is why, as we have discovered, every virtue is bracketed by two vices, to remind us that virtue is found in the interaction between two opposites. Here the virtue of courage is surrounded by cowardice and rashness. With the support of others, Elizabeth found her way to the virtuous middle.

North American culture is fed by and feeds on hundreds of different fears and anxieties, both collective and individual. Witness the tremendous amount of time, money, and effort spent at every level of society on security, defense, and protection against known and unknown forces. This can encompass the fear of aging, of illness, the foreigner, poverty, criminals, other religions, nations, or lifestyles. Fear is a more specific phenomenon, while anxiety is free-floating and generalized. Rather than giving in to the fear or anxiety, face it. Willigis Jäger offers this helpful insight in *Search for the Meaning of Life*:

> We should repress nothing. What is there is there. Look at it, accept it, let it come! Make friends with your fear and your rage. They belong to you. After all, you don't cut off your toe if it hurts.

Try this some time with sadness: accept it, but don't wallow in it. Don't make a big deal about it. Look at it....

Let's consider the same with anxiety. So many of us are plagued by anxiety, but we don't know why. We don't know where it comes from or where it hides itself. We can say "yes" to anxiety. We can say, "yes, I am afraid." We can take it into our exercise. When we repress anxiety or sadness, these emotions will disguise themselves and hide in some corner of our psyche. Then, when they pop up, they appear with a totally different face, perhaps as aggression, pride, or even virtue, which can deceive us even further.

If we don't want to fall victim to this subtle trick, we have to realize that sadness, jealousy, aggression, and so on, belong to the psychic energy of our personality structure and hence to our life, and that ultimately they are as much expression of the Divine as joy, peace, and harmony. Everything we let be has the tendency to change into something pleasant. But the things we fight grab onto us. (142–43)

Your fears are the gateway to courage and deeper self-knowledge. It is this deepening insight that brings light to the darkness. Without this work, there is no revelation, no clarity, and we are doomed to mindless repetitions or obsessions. We can be grateful for the poet Dante's brilliant suggestion that the difference between purgatory and hell is the light of insight. It is insight that can begin to liberate us from repetitive patterns of thought, feeling, and/or behavior. To approach life with an open, nonjudgmental attitude is to create space for internal freedom. We can accept that anything and everyone can be our teacher, that indeed, we are not alone on this journey of individuation. With the right attitude and perspective, we can see that in some way, everything is meant to assist us on the ever-challenging journey called life.

Negative emotions have a good deal to teach us. To leave this place of revelation too soon is to miss the rich interior message of the particular emotion. What is the real message inside the fear, the loneliness, the anger, the sadness? I find that it helps to create an unfinished sentence in my journal such as "What I am really afraid of is...or I am sad about...or

I am angry that…." Wisdom and insight often come simply and slowly, like an unveiling of a beautiful painting. Pastoral theologian Evelyn Whitehead uses the helpful image of a ship in a still harbor. Imagine the ship as your negative emotion coming into the still harbor of your focused attention but don't let it set anchor. Give it the necessary time but don't let it control your life in an obsessive fashion. As Jäger points out, "We practice pure observation, pure attentiveness, without any evaluation or preoccupation. Emotions must be lived—even welcomed—steadfastly and imperturbably. No commentary, no getting swept away, no distorting. Feeling is like a cloud that moves across the blue sky; it may darken the sky, but it never stays" (142–43).

Stillness is a necessary pause in the ongoing creation of my personhood. Perhaps this is why Psalm 46:10 offers the gentle, but urgent invitation, "Be still, and know that I am God." The Book of Genesis (2:2–3) tells us that stillness is built into the fabric of creation. The stillness of a lake allows the silt to settle so that clarity is possible. So it is when we still the worrisome negative thoughts that plague us each day. A series of simple deep breaths can center us and once again remind us of our embodiment. Fears and anxieties proliferate in the mind and can often be settled by an exercise of reconnection with the body. I know of a psychologist who teaches patients who suffer from anxiety the basic techniques of breathing. At first glance, this might seem basic, even facile, yet it is the kind of regular practice that can truly help us to remain centered in our humanity. We know that what makes music melodious and memorable is the space between the notes, rather than the notes themselves. Stillness is the spaciousness that opens us up to multiple possibilities and choices. Years ago, at a dream conference attended by a large number of psychoanalysts, one professional shared a very dark and foreboding dream experienced by one of his clients. The conference participants waited for the main speaker, Carl Jung's grandson, to respond with an eloquent insight into the dream's message. He surprised them with a request. He asked them to stand in silence for a few moments to honor the dream. After he sat down, he explained that some dreams are best honored in silence rather than through interpretation.

Stillness brings to possibility an artistic rendering of our life. It is the darkness, and the dark colors, that make the light so beautiful. Thus, it is through the experience of suffering that we can appreciate the moments of great joy. As St. Thomas More said, "God came not to suppress suffering, nor even to explain it, but to fill it with his [sic] presence." It is in the indwelling of our own most precious lives that we discover Ultimate Mystery. Being consciously still is becoming present to the Presence within. Perhaps this is why there are so many stories of "conversion" from persons who have experienced monastic enclosure, or the trial of imprisonment or a long convalescence. The English poet David Whyte captures this change in his eloquent way: "Revelation must be terrible / knowing you can / never hide your voice again" ("Revelation Must Be Terrible")

Revelation comes in many shapes and forms, but it most commonly comes through the experience of stillness in one form or another. In Mark 4:35–41, we read of Jesus calming the storm after his sleep in the boat. The still calm of his interior life is projected onto external reality. The disciples are caught up in the terror of the situation because they have lost perspective, hence Jesus' words of rebuke to them: "Why are you afraid? Have you still no faith?" They do not have an interior stillness, or anchor, and so their terror feeds upon itself. Stillness helps to liberate us from the controlling clutches of fear and anxiety. Many people turn to religion only in dire circumstances or in moral dilemmas. Authentic faith and therefore, energizing spirituality, is meant to engage every nook and cranny of our lives; otherwise it can devolve into superstition or a toxic comfort system.

How do you calm yourself, or still the incessant voices that cry out to be addressed? Some people find that a cup of tea in the middle of the afternoon helps, or perhaps a short nap. Deep breathing is a quick and easy way to remind ourselves of our humanity, our presence in the moment. Choosing not to answer a text message or a cell phone call right away is a helpful discipline that can aid us in taking charge of our busy lives, so that we are not caught in the maelstrom that requires immediate reaction to the demands and expectations of others.

Prayer is a traditional form of responding to the interior yearnings of the human soul. There are five different categories of prayer as various ways of expressing this inner hunger:

- Informal or spontaneous
- Petitionary or intercessional
- Liturgical or ritualistic
- Meditative or contemplative
- Communion or "feeling" (Bourgeault)

Stillness is akin to the single camera image that holds the memory of an event. The image does not completely capture everything about the event but it does intensify and bring alive the encounter in a way that is poignant. As American poet Mary Oliver wisely says, "Sometimes I need only to stand wherever I am to be blessed" ("It was early," *Evidence*, 21). Stillness both highlights and underscores the events of our lives, as it offers us a frame for viewing who and where we are in the great mystery of God.

QUESTIONS

What brings you to your still point?

When are you most anxious or fearful?

What have you learned from your fears?

PRAYER FORMS

Contemplation: Practice pure nonjudgmental observation of what's going on around you and within you. Let it be.

Focusing: A guided prayer practice that puts the emphasis on our feelings in our bodies. It asks us to listen to our body knowledge rather than simply our intellectual perceptions.

Contemplative walk: Walk slowly and deliberately, aware of the sensory stimuli around you and the internal noise as well.

SPIRITUAL PRACTICES

Daily examen: A technique of prayerful reflection on the events of the day in order to detect God's presence and discern God's direction for us. Developed by St. Ignatius of Loyola, this method involves five steps:

1. Become aware of God's presence;
2. Review the day with gratitude;
3. Pay attention to your emotions;
4. Choose one feature from your day (positive or negative) and pray from it;
5. Look toward tomorrow, asking God's guidance.

Deep breathing: Slowly inhale the breath and hold it. Let it go. Do this five times.

Massage: Gently massage your head, hands, or feet.

FURTHER READING

Hollis, James. *Finding Meaning in the Second Half of Life: How to Finally, Really Grow Up.* New York: Gotham Books, 2005.

Mayers, Gregory. *Listen to the Desert: Secrets of Spiritual Maturity from the Desert Fathers and Mothers.* Liguori, MO: Liguori Publications, 1996.

Sardello, Robert. *The Power of the Soul: Living the Twelve Virtues.* Charlottesville, VA: Hampton Roads, 2002.

Steindl-Rast, David. *A Listening Heart: The Art of Contemplative Living.* New York: Crossroad, 1983.

13

Surrender
I Give Up!

(Control/Autonomy)

Once upon a time, a stream was working itself across the country, experiencing little difficulty, for it simply ran around the rocks and through the mountains and forests. Then one day it arrived at a desert. Just as it had crossed every other barrier, the stream tried to cross this one, but it found that as fast as it ran into the sand, its waters disappeared. After many, many attempts it became very discouraged; it appeared that there was no way it could continue the journey. Then a voice came in the wind. "If you stay the way you are, you cannot cross the sands; you cannot become more than a quagmire. To go further, you will have to lose yourself." "But If I lose myself," the stream cried, "I will never know what I'm supposed to be." "Quite the contrary," said the voice, "if you lose yourself, you will become more than you ever dreamed you could be." So the stream surrendered to the dying sun. And the clouds into which it was formed were carried by the raging wind for many miles. Once it crossed the desert, the stream poured down from the skies, fresh and clean, and full of the energy that comes from the storms. (Bausch, 351)

TO SURRENDER IS NOT a "manly" thing to do in any culture. We often see it as a sign of failure or weakness. However, to yield or submit to the inevitable or the necessary truth is one half of the equation; the other is to take responsibility for your life, to make it happen. This is the deep wisdom of the cosmos and of the mystics who know the Creator's ways. You cannot give away that which you do not have, but once you have it, you must give it up or turn it over to a higher power. This is the work of the creature in the face of the Creator's wisdom. There will always be a tension between holding on and letting go. This is the rhythm of the cosmos. We see this flow happen daily in the many interactions of our lives, from merging into a busy line of traffic, to the conversational back-and-forth exchange of words, to the sunset of yet another day. Nothing new happens without letting go of the last good thing.

We cannot accept this truth or relax into it unless we know a greater love. One of the words used most often in the writings of the mystics in describing God's presence is "floating." To float in God's love is our vocation, our calling; to trust that there is a "great enough" Power to hold us in that frightening interim between letting go and landing on something new. We see this most clearly in the action of the trapeze artist who has to let go of one set of handholds in order to reach out and receive another set. The "in-between space" is the surrendering to the unknown, the possible. Letting go of the need to control the outcome is perhaps one of the most difficult things we are asked to do as believers. This is what is called faith. We really don't want faith; we want certainty. We want to know, without a doubt, that our plans will materialize in exactly the way we have planned. We want to be protected from pain, not to go through it. Yet this is what real faith does for us: it helps us through the pain of the moment, the week, the years of growing into our full humanity.

It takes courage to lean into the pain of our lives, but we must do this if we are to know true freedom. The process of leaning into the pain will transform us. Years ago, I injured my shoulder in a bicycle accident. As part of my rehabilitation, I worked with a physiotherapist. One day, when I was struggling to do the prescribed exercise correctly, he said, "You have to lean into the pain. That is the only way you will get better." Those words struck me as being true for my life as well. When I lean away from pain through denial, avoidance, or escapism, I cheat myself from growing in maturity and authentic happiness. As you work through the pain of therapy, illness, or recovery from an accident, it takes courage to see that this event is a snapshot of how you do life. Is it working for you? If not, what needs to change?

When you let go of the outcome, the plan, or the situation, it inevitably returns to you in a surprising new way. This reminds us that we see only a small part of the overall picture of our lives, let alone reality. Only God sees the whole picture, and God seems to be quite all right with reality as it is. Our task is to live in harmony with the Creator's cosmos, trusting the process and God's way of doing things. This is the antithesis of living with a controlling attitude toward life, always fearful of what the next moment or encounter may bring. This attitude can then lead to an autonomous way of living, separate from anyone else, building our own tower, so to speak. Rather than living such a willful existence, we are to surrender with willing acceptance to what is right in front of us. As Gerald May says,

> Willingness implies a surrendering of one's self-separateness, an entering-into, an immersion in the deepest processes of life itself. It is a realization that one already is a part of some ultimate cosmic process and it is a commitment to participation in that process. In contrast, willfulness is the setting of oneself apart from the fundamental essence of life in an attempt to master, direct, control, or otherwise manipulate existence. More simply, willingness is saying yes to the mystery of being alive in each moment. Willfulness is saying no, or perhaps more commonly, "Yes, but…." (*Will and Spirit*, 6)

To surrender to someone or something else is the antithesis of control. To turn over our sense of control willingly is to trust that a greater Love constantly holds us, teaches us, and guides us, almost in spite of ourselves. Therefore, we are to surrender to the grace that is already there even before we have asked for it. The material for this "awakening" is the reality of our lives. Jesus is a model for this process of awakening and responding to the mystery of our lives. He lived the disarmed life, accepting what came with love and compassion, all the while pondering the mystery of the unfolding events of his life. This is also what we are to do:

actively enter the dance of our *own* life and ponder the significance within the depths of the ordinary daily activities of our existence. From this centered place of meaning, we then respond with love and compassion toward others.

But before there is a breakthrough into something new, there often is a breakdown of some sort or another. This is necessary, to make space for the fresh creation. Think of a remodeling project, or cleaning out closet. One must start with "destruction" or the tossing out of the "unwanted" first, before beginning to recreate. There is an amusing story about a busy career woman who was preparing to move to a new residence. She had hired a professional moving company to assist her in this daunting task. When the workers arrived, they asked what she wanted to pack. With a wave of her arm indicating all the stuff around her, she said, "Everything!" And so they did! When she arrived at her new place, she discovered that the movers had taken her literally. Along with her furniture and appliances, they had neatly packed her rubbish! (Bausch, 292). In Luke 9:24, we read Jesus' words to his disciples: "For those who want to save their life will lose it, and those who lose their life for my sake will save it." Losing and saving operate in tandem. They are not oppositional.

In religious television programming, we often see people giving public testimony to the work of God in their lives. Inevitably, one will say something like this: "I didn't know happiness until I finally surrendered my life to Christ." What they are saying in ordinary language is that they learned the secret of letting go of an attachment, of turning their own power over to a Higher Power. It is like taking a deep breath and then letting it go. To hold onto the breath just leads to discomfort or in the extreme, passing out. Alternatively, this might be seen as a kind of spiritual constipation.

To surrender to the cosmic dance of "turning it over to the Lord" is a very liberating experience. At first glance, it appears that this is nothing more than being irresponsible. On the contrary, this is a cooperative venture between you and your Creator. God will do God's part, but you must do your part. It is an interactive exercise that changes with the situation. Think about the recent phenomenon of extreme sports, and the reports of those who engage in them. These people talk about their experiences in exuberant, passionate words. They speak about the adrenaline rush and the letting-go experience afterward that leads to an ecstatic euphoria. This is not unlike the experience of religious people who describe their conversion encounter with God. The Creator's wisdom is hidden in all aspects of creation, especially in our own lives, no matter how we name it.

Your identity is hidden in God. You are God's beloved. This truth is both a gift and a responsibility. It is a gift in that it is freely given; you have not earned it. It is your responsibility to live from this place of being unconditionally loved. When we don't, we become beastly or robotic, objectifying others and abusing creation. To live from this place, called "home" in the truest sense of the word, is to live in the Now, the Eternal. The real work of the spiritual life is to "dis-identify" from anything that is not authentic about our nature, our essence. For example, you are not your thoughts, your feelings, your belongings, or your job. You are bigger than this! You are God's beloved, pure and simple. So let go of spending so much time giving credence or power to these passing things of the world. To lose this false sense of yourself is to find your True Self in God.

This work is best summarized in John 12:24: "Very truly, I tell you, unless a grain of wheat falls into the earth and dies, it remains just a single grain; but if it dies, it bears much fruit." Dying and rising to a new way of life is at the heart of the Christian message. Nothing truly new will ever happen unless we surrender or hand over that which has become a blockage. Does the seed really know what it will be like to achieve its full potentiality? Does the caterpillar really "know" what it will be like to be a butterfly? Does a child really know what life will be like outside the womb? No, of course not, but nature responds to the wisdom of the Creator and moves this seamless process forward. When we, as conscious beings, fight this process of surrendering to transformation, we suffer needlessly. To accept this process and actively participate in the unfolding mystery of our own unique life is to be truly free and alive. In a paradoxical way, this prepares us for death. As mythologist Joseph Campbell says, "We must be willing to let go of the life we have planned, so as to have the life that is waiting for us."

The lessons of life are intertwined with the lessons of death. To live well means to live with an attitude and practice of holding on (receiving) and letting go (surrendering) appropriately. This is the eternal will of God that is embedded in creation and lived out in the lives of mature believers. As Teresa of Avila said, "We can only learn to know ourselves and do what we can, namely, surrender our will and fulfil God's will in us."

QUESTIONS

What do you need to surrender to God?

What names you or claims you as a human being?

Where are you most controlling in your life?

PRAYER FORMS

Prayer of the imagination: Close your eyes and place your hands on your lap, palms up. Relax your whole body. Focus on what is blocking you from being free or at peace. Is it a thought, a feeling, or a relationship? Once you have connected with the source of your discomfort, place your emotions into your hands and close them tightly. Feel the tension or the turmoil. Breathe into the feeling. Now let the breath go. Again. Breathe in. Breathe out. As you slowly are able to let your attachment to this tension go, open your hands.

Surrender: Surrender your life to God in a heartfelt way.

Labyrinth: A walking meditation using a nonlinear pathway to lead you to the center where you are invited to release your burden, returning refreshed and renewed.

Desire prayer: Use all your senses to create in your imagination a scene that depicts what you deeply yearn for and then pray in and through that desire. Let go of specific outcomes, handing it over to God in the process.

SPIRITUAL PRACTICES

Tonglen: A four-step process of focused breathing in and breathing out, taking in pain/suffering and sending out spaciousness and relief.

Acceptance: Accept the things you cannot change.

Share the secrets: Share your secrets with a trusted friend or counselor, perhaps taking a fearless moral inventory of your life with that person.

Forgiveness: Let go of blaming yourself/others for past mistakes, poor choices, or destructive behavior.

Dream work: Record, interpret, and reflect on the meaning of your dreams. Then respond to them.

FURTHER READING

Chodron, Pema. *Start Where You Are: A Guide to Compassionate Living.* Boston: Shambhala, 2004.

May, Gerald G. *Will and Spirit: A Contemplative Psychology.* San Francisco: Harper & Row, 1982.

Richo, David. *The Five Things We Cannot Change…and the Happiness We Find by Embracing Them.* Boston: Shambhala, 2006.

Rohr, Richard. *Breathing Under Water: Spirituality and the Twelve Steps.* Cincinnati: St. Anthony Messenger Press, 2011.

————. *The Naked Now: Learning to See as the Mystics See.* New York: Crossroad, 2009.

14

Support
We're All in This Together
(Elitism/Xenophobia)

CONTEMPORARY WESTERN SOCIETY seems to experience a real tension between the spirit of independence on the one hand, and the notion of dependence on the other. Whether it is presented in movies, politics, or religion, independence is portrayed as a worthy goal and dependence is often demeaned as laziness or lack of will. A life-giving spirituality holds up a third, more viable, option—interdependence.

A spirit of interdependence acknowledges at its core that we are all connected. No one is completely independent or dependent. We all have aspects of our lives where we experience independence or dependence. For example, while you may live alone, earning your own income, cooking and cleaning for yourself, you almost certainly did not make all your own clothing, grow your own food, or create your own entertainment. You have relied upon the expertise of others to contribute to your well-being.

Interdependence also presumes and encourages healthy boundaries between and among individuals, family, community, and strangers. This is about cultivating healthy respect for oneself and others (Luke 6:31). Dependency can often lead to codependent behavior, while independency sometimes leads to aloofness and elitism.

In the Divine Wisdom, dependency and independency interface to remind us that we need each other, like two halves of a whole. Our needs, and the needs of those around us, can sometimes work in us in surprising ways. The story of Amanda is illustrative.

Amanda was a young, brand-new elementary school teacher who wanted desperately to do things right for "her" children. One of her young students, Vicky, had only one arm, and Amanda was very conscious of including her in all classroom activities, without calling attention to her obvious limitation. One day, Amanda taught the students a new song that included hand motions and clapping. As the children exuberantly joined in the singing of the song, and began the clapping, she suddenly realized she had forgotten about Vicky's limitation. She found herself unable to look directly at Vicky, so mortified did she feel. Eventually, however, she surreptitiously stole a glance in her direction and was delighted to see that another girl had crossed the aisle and was clapping with Vicky. The scene was truly liberating for Amanda. In a flash, she realized that this is how God generally responds to our needs—through others.

We are created in communion for community. Some of our deepest joys occur when we experience this sense of union or right relationship. Is it any wonder, then, that historically, human beings have bonded together in groups, communities, and fellowships for support, encouragement, and assistance? In this communal environment, participants regularly encounter their own hidden strengths and weaknesses through the mirror of the lives of others. This same principle is at work when we encounter the stranger, the foreigner, and the outcast. When we refuse to receive compassionately that which is different or strange, we might miss the opportunity for growth and possible enrichment. What type of communion really matters to Jesus?

The support that can assist you in your own spiritual growth is the kind of attitude that trusts you will be given what you need for the journey ahead (Mark 6:8–13). There is no fast tracking in the development of relationships and communication. Choosing a specific group of persons to whom we decide to be accountable grounds us in the certainty that we are not alone and reminds us of our place of equality in the human family. These chosen individuals witness to our innate goodness, and call out the best of our personhood as we wrestle our inner "demons." They remind us of our authentic nature as a beloved daughter/son of God. At the same time, these people should not be afraid to stand with us in our struggles. We can hope and trust that they will not shrink in fear or diminish their commitment to us.

My own professional support group of priests has been with me for many years. These men have helped me with my struggles of self-doubt, ecclesial missteps, and ministerial challenges. I cannot imagine how different my life would be without them. Their honesty, compassion, encouragement, and directness have been refreshingly helpful with my own growth as a man, and as a priest.

My small personal support group is made up of people from widely diverging walks in life. Three of them are from cultures and countries different from my own. I have found these men and women to be a priceless presence and influence in my own growth and healing process. They have mirrored to me my own goodness and compassionately supported me in facing my blind spots and darkness. Whether in person, through Skype, online, or through a phone call, I turn to them to assist me in remaining grounded in my humanity. Who supports you and encourages you in your life?

Many people with addictive/compulsive tendencies and behaviors have found great support in groups that follow twelve-step programs. Other groups are available for people who are temporarily struggling with a particular aspect of their life such as bereavement, financial problems, or psychological issues. Approaching this type of support with humility and appropriate vulnerability enriches the experience and enables authentic healing and growth to occur. Do you know how to ask for support?

Supporting other peoples' new ideas, innovations, and creative solutions to difficult issues is another way of opening ourselves to the process of strengthening the interior life. The gospel way to resolve conflicts is by focusing on common concerns and working to support those seeking the common good. Often we can resort to stereotyping those who disagree with us; this allows us to remain frozen in place, feeling self-righteous. Thomas Aquinas offered this wisdom: "We must love whose opinions we share, and those we disagree with, because both have labored in their search for truth."

This kind of "support" is often more difficult, and more challenging, than simply "being there" for someone in need; it challenges us to let go, when appropriate, of our own need to win, or dominate, or be right. In other words, support is called for in a wide variety of situations, and can sometimes take surprising forms.

QUESTIONS

How do you respond to those who are different from you?

Do you seek out and develop friendships with persons from other cultures and ways of life?

To whom do you turn for support and encouragement?

How might you encourage others in their life journey?

PRAYER FORMS

Prayer partner. Regularly meeting with someone who will pray with you and for you.

Prayer group: Join a group of people who gather regularly to pray.

Prayer for one's enemies: Our enemies are the best revealers of our shadow side. Praying compassionately for them can release us from toxic resentment.

SPIRITUAL PRACTICES

Small group sharing: Create or join a group that focuses on a theme of your interest.

Mentoring/coaching: Seek out someone who can guide you in areas you want to develop and nurture (for example, exercise, computer use, art, music).

Therapy: A commitment to honestly, humbly look at any emotional blockages, and to make some real changes for your betterment, is a sign of spiritual maturity.

Scripture or theological book study group: A weekly or monthly gathering around a specific book or chapter in Scripture can support your growth in the spiritual life.

Meaningful questions/discussions at evening mealtimes: Choose a question or theme for a thoughtful mealtime discussion.

Develop an open and accepting attitude toward those who are different from you: As a global citizen, what can you learn from the stranger, the foreigner, and the outcast? These can be some of the best of teachers for our spiritual growth.

FURTHER READING

Armstrong, Karen. *Twelve Steps to a Compassionate Life.* New York: Anchor Books, 2010.

Richo, David. *How to Be an Adult in Relationships: The Five Keys to Mindful Loving.* Boston: Shambhala, 2002.

Wallis, Jim. *God's Politics: A New Vision for Faith and Politics in America.* New York: HarperCollins, 2005.

Wicks, Robert J. *Crossing the Desert: Learning to Let Go, See Clearly, and Live Simply.* Notre Dame, IN: Sorin Books, 2007.

15

Sustenance
What Must I Do to Survive?

(Aridity/Darkness)

WHAT SHOULD I DO WHEN I am going through a period of darkness? How do I cope in times of aridity in prayer? What about those of us who feel like we are praying into a void? I feel lost; what's wrong with me? These and other similar questions fill the hearts and minds of many of us post-modern individuals at times, and for some people, over a long period. You are not alone! One woman friend of mine calls herself a "believer in exile" because she feels deeply alienated by the current state of her Church, and, as a consequence, feels separated from God. These questions are impor-tant, and are not to be dismissed with pious remedies (just keep praying harder), or with platitudes (God is always with you), however helpful they might seem. They are questions of depth and honest searching. They are not about doubt, although that is a healthy ingredient for any thinking believer. Doubt and confusion can often serve as an entrée into the deep-ening of our faith, encouraging us to look elsewhere or to trust the dark-ness. The antithesis of faith is not doubt; it is apathy—the lack of will to stay in the struggle to grow. Merton affirms this: "You cannot be a person of faith unless you know how to doubt" (*New Seeds*, 77).

Sometimes it is painful even to be around family or friends who have had powerful religious experiences or spiritual "revelations." Their experiences and newfound fervor can feel like a judgment on your own lack of a felt divine encounter. Often we can assume that they are more spiritual than we are, and have greater authority to speak about all things divine. This doesn't help, especially when we hear from certain religious "experts" who want to blame our lack on some unrepented sin or unacknowledged shortcoming. *Wrong!* God is not punishing you or hiding from you. God desires an intimate relationship with you. God always and everywhere reaches out to us in a whole range of different ways. Recognition of this variety is important. We are created equally, yes, but quite uniquely. Our way of experiencing God is singular depending upon personality, life circumstance, experience, education, and openness to the unknown. We don't earn God's love or attention. We are freely given this gift by our existence.

Many years ago, my uncle Tim was a Trappist monk at Our Lady of the Holy Trinity monastery in Huntsville, Utah. He had faithfully followed all the rules and disciplines of his monastic vows and had generally felt very satisfied with his faith. In 1968, the community began to receive many college-age visitors who spoke of having had a powerful religious experience that they referred to as the "baptism in the Holy Spirit." Tim noticed that these young people had received many amazing charismatic gifts and seemed to exude a beautiful aura of spiritual maturity that was beyond their years. He felt jealous and told the Lord so. "I have spent my adult life as a Trappist monk, giving up meat, getting up early to pray, working hard on the farm, and I haven't experienced these kinds of gifts, or the fruits of the Spirit that they talk about. What's going on?" Tim waited quite a while for an answer. Finally, he sensed God gently chiding him, "Tim, which do you prefer: justice or mercy?" Tim really had to mull over that question and its implications. After a while, he finally said, "Lord, I want your mercy. I give you all my fasting, prayers, and the fruits of my hard manual labor. You don't owe me anything. Just give me your gifts to glorify you." It was then that Tim noticed a "relaxing" in his spirit and he was finally able to receive God's unique gifts for him.

Tim learned a very important lesson through this experience. None of us can earn God's love. God loves us because God is good, not because we are good. This Divine Love is then manifested in an individual way for each one of us according to our needs, not necessarily according to our desires. Often we are tempted to believe that God only loves us or demonstrates that love when things are going well for us. This is not true at all. Remember the temptations that Jesus faced in the desert (Matt 4)? These are the most common temptations of every human being. In each instance, Jesus refuses to lose his grounding and remains centered in his identity as the Beloved of God. In the first temptation, he is offered the creaturely comfort of food, but he knows that when physical comfort is removed from his life, Abba has not abandoned him. In the second temptation, Jesus is offered the social support of angels to protect him from pain. He acknowledges that God does not cause pain or try to shield us from the struggle of the human condition; rather, God sits with us in our pain. In the third temptation, Jesus is offered all earthly power. Jesus sees through the emptiness of power, prestige, and possessions and recognizes his own true authority as Beloved Son. These temptations hovered around him throughout his life, just as they do for us.

We know that faith trusts the unseen, the mystery of the unknown, believing that it is good, despite the external signs. But when we are in a dark place, we need a lighthouse on the rocky coast we are negotiating, to give us some sense of "thereness"; some sense of clarity and direction. Who or what does this for you? Is there a person in your life to whom you can relate, who has a rock solid faith but can accommodate your struggles? Is there an author you have found who can speak to your searchings? For some people it might be someone like Henri Nouwen, Joan Chittister, Kathleen Norris, or Michael Morwood. For others, it might be someone more traditional like Augustine or John of the Cross.

Most books on spirituality have been written by intuitive-feeling persons. Their approach is authentic and helpful for many but not for everyone. What about the thinkers and sensates among us who have different needs or ways of connecting with God? Are we any less capable of learning how to grow in the spiritual life or to have "spiritual experiences"? Of course not. It's similar to learning a new language. We need to learn how God speaks differently to the occasion and to the person. Perhaps it might be helpful for you to look at some contemporary personality profiling tools that might help you better understand your own way of approaching life. To that end, you may like to look at the Myers-Briggs Type Indicator, which focuses on personal preferences, or the Enneagram, which concentrates on inner motivations, or the Spiritual Strengths Finder, which is a personalized analysis tool devised by Dr. Richard Johnson that identifies one's core strengths. All or any of these can be helpful in discerning your own interior way of connecting with God or "things spiritual."

The great need here is for sustenance.

Sustenance can often come from the most unlikely places. Sometimes it will come in the form of shared suffering with others. Other times it will come through simply being in the beauty of creation, or perhaps through synchronistic events. In the Book of Judges, we read the story of Elijah, who was looking for inspiration in a time of great disheartenment and vulnerability. God responded in a way Elijah least expected, but which he certainly understood—through the forces of creation. In Exodus, we read of Moses being allowed to see only the back of God. It is certain that for some, the experience of God's language is found in hindsight rather than foresight or insight. In John's Gospel, we read of Peter's concern for John and what is going to happen to him. Jesus bluntly tells him to mind his own business and look to his own task. We each have a different call, a unique way of experiencing the Divine.

Some people feel that they have no sense of God's presence in their lives. In prayer, it's as if they are speaking, but God is not responding, in any way, shape, or form. Here's the problem: prayer is for our sake, not for God's. It is not about cajoling or making a deal with God in order to get what we want. Prayer serves to remind us that we are not God, nor are we a machine, and that we are not animals. We have a conscious task to grow into the fullness of our humanity, a divinizing process. Prayer assists us in this necessary work by recalling our spiritual nature. We are much more than our ideas, feelings, social networks, physical makeup, or the external trappings of our lives. Prayer is about bringing all of ourselves to God as we know God.

This journey of prayer is no guarantee that we will receive what we ask for. We often get what we need in life, not always what we want. It is only through genuine reflection that we can see this more clearly, usually with hindsight. Thomas Merton put it this way: "We have what we seek, it is there all the time, and if we give it time, it will make itself known to us." Think of John of the Cross and his lengthy dark night of suffering at the hands of his religious community, or Teresa of Calcutta and her life-time of interior darkness at prayer, or Thérèse of Lisieux and her great doubts in the last year of her short life. The spiritual nourishment that we all seek is not a promise, as much as it is a by-product of living an authentic life of integrity.

In arid Western Australia, there are more varieties of flora than anywhere else in the world. Naturalists tell us the reason for this is because no one species has had the opportunity to control the environment. In these relatively dry, desolate conditions with no volcanic activity and poor soil conditions, there is a plethora of life. Similarly, we discover in the Scriptures the same basic truth. In times and places of aridity, life springs forth and persists against the odds. Walter Brueggemann finds in the Hebrew Scriptures a noticeable pattern for God's people. First, they find themselves securely oriented for a time, then painfully disoriented, and finally surprisingly reoriented. This pattern is repeated so often that it is seen as the norm for life. Is it possible that your times of aridity and darkness, whether for a time or for a lifetime, are snapshots of the larger picture of what it means to be a creature in this cosmos?

Some people feel abandoned in times of grief and loss. For others the "absence" of God is a long-term, otherwise inexplicable experience. The fact is, in times of aridity, emptiness, and darkness, God is closer to you than you are to yourself. God uses this period as a time of interior "stretching or expanding" of our experience of the unknown. This happens most often through the arena of our greatest weakness. Joseph Campbell offers this bit of wisdom: "It is by going down into the abyss that we recover the treasure of life. Where you stumble, there is your treasure." How are we to respond? Whether it is in times of trauma or pain, a prevailing mood, or a constant day in and day out wrenching affair—the response should be the same. We need to look at the three arenas of personal physiological makeup, social networks, and intellectual understanding.

To sustain ourselves for the long haul, we must be ruthlessly honest and committed to a way of discipline. Here are some helpful ideas:

1. Seek out a mature supportive community.
2. Read intellectually stimulating books and materials.

3. Meet regularly with a spiritual director or guide.
4. Observe your self-talk and make any necessary changes.
5. Seek out external encouragement.
6. Regularly do something meaningful and tangible for others.
7. Daily acknowledge your body through some physical expression.
8. Pray often.

Anyone can pilot a boat in calm waters; it takes a courageous and determined person to negotiate the storms that our own small craft will inevitably encounter as we make our way home to God. We discover who we are through this life-sustaining work.

QUESTIONS

How do you respond to times of aridity in prayer?

What assists you in difficult times of darkness or doubt?

How do you experience God's presence or absence?

PRAYER FORMS

Centering prayer: Focus on one word or image for 10–20 minutes.

Prayer through creation: Place yourself in the midst of creation and pray "through" one creative element (for example, a tree, the ocean, a plant, an animal, or bird). Have a conversation with the element.

Journaling: Write in a journal your reflections, poems, drawings, dream interpretations to express your emotions.

SPIRITUAL PRACTICES

Make a pilgrimage: Visit a place that will console or uplift you.

Participate in volunteer work: Give your time to someone or some group that is in desperate circumstances.

Seek out spiritual direction: Don't go it alone. Regularly meet with a wise, spiritually mature person.

Release: Practice letting go or surrendering the undue attachments in your life; accept the necessary losses of life.

FURTHER READING

Green, Thomas. *When the Well Runs Dry: Prayer Beyond the Beginnings.* Notre Dame, IN: Ave Maria Press, 1998.

May, Gerald. *The Dark Night of the Soul: A Psychiatrist Explores the Connection Between Darkness and Spiritual Growth.* New York: HarperCollins, 2004.

Morwood, Michael. *Faith, Hope, and a Bird Called George: A Spiritual Fable.* New London, CT: Twenty-Third Publications, 2011.

Remen, Rachel Naomi. *Kitchen Table Wisdom: Stories That Heal.* New York: Riverhead Books 1996.

Wicks, Robert. *Riding the Dragon: 10 Lessons for Inner Strength in Challenging Times.* Notre Dame, IN: Sorin Books, 2003.

16

Source of Income
Paying the Bills—
Blood, Sweat, and Tears
(Boredom/Willfulness)

MANY YEARS AGO, my father and I were walking along the beach and I asked him, "What is the one lesson that you wanted to pass on to your children?" I was struck by his immediate and passionate response, "An honest day's work for an honest day's pay!" Many of us have grown up with this idea, but with all the changes in the work environment and job market, does this maxim still apply? What value was placed on work in your family?

Work is a key component of human fulfillment and the building up of self-esteem (Gen 2:15). It allows people to fulfill their total vocation by "drawing us out of ourselves, and at the same time, makes us more of what we are meant to be" (Chittister, *Labor Day*). Ideally, our work is based on our dignity as human beings. In some way, work should satisfy one's soul as well as one's physical needs. To be trapped in soulless work is truly difficult, and surely, it is the task of society to find ways to make such work less burdensome. When work becomes exploitative rather than liberating, then we are talking about human desecration. As French author and philosopher Albert Camus said, "Without work all life grows rotten. But when work is soulless, life stifles and dies." The way back to satisfying, pleasurable work is to collaborate with God. Following the example of Jesus, the Benedictine monks live their lives according to the maxim "prayer and work" (*ora et labora*). Joining the spiritual and material world together on the altar of their daily labor creates a natural rhythm of relatedness and integration. An Egyptian proverb puts it succinctly: The rower reaches shore partly by pulling, partly by letting go.

As with any human activity, we are always tempted to move between the extremes of passivity or frenetic activity. Neither of these serves the ultimate good of the person or the community. When I was an adolescent, my brother Tony and I spent the summer with my Trappist uncle, Tim, at the Monastery of Our Lady of the Holy Trinity in Utah. We had been given the task of washing the guest dishes. One afternoon we had just started the process when two young men walked into the kitchen and just stood watching us in silence. When we had just about completed our task, the older of the two men stepped forward and asked if they could help. Totally flummoxed by their actions, we simply looked at each other and thought, "What gives?" The next morning we asked Tim who these men were, and he chuckled and said, "Oh those guys belong to a 'super spiritual group' that does absolutely nothing without asking God what to do. They were standing there asking God if they should volunteer their help!" Many people refuse to move on something until they get a clear direction from God. However, when the need is obvious and immediate, and there is no one else around to help, then normally, God has sent someone—*you*!

Many people, on the other hand, struggle with work overload, addiction, or overwhelming stress. The antidote to high levels of stress in an adult is a reconnection with the healthy inner child. The enviable functions of that inner child are the very activities often missing from the life of the overwhelmed adult. These include, but are not limited to:

- Engagement with Creation (water, wind, sunshine, animals, soil, plants)
- Embrace of the Imagination (games, daydreaming, humor, stories)
- Love of Play (spontaneity, swings, flying kites, building sandcastles, walking barefoot)
- Ability to Fantasize (songs, dance, art, curiosity)

- Capacity for Contemplation (focus on one thing, awe)
- Openness to the idea of the Group (friends, family)

Work is to be a means of self-expression and cocreation, like God's work, to contribute to the relatedness of society and to offer a reconciling function. In this way we work for earthly progress and the development of the kingdom of God. For Christians, this translates theologically into participating in the cross and resurrection of Christ.

"Whatever your task, put yourselves into it, as done for the Lord and not for your masters, since you know that from the Lord you will receive the inheritance as your reward" (Col 3:23–24). This understanding is colorfully portrayed in the story of the woodcarver, as retold by Thomas Merton:

Khing, the master carver, made a bell stand
Of precious wood. When it was finished,
All who saw it were astounded. They said it must be
The work of spirits.
The Prince of Lu said to the master carver:
"What is your secret?"

Khing replied: "I am only a workman:
I have no secret. There is only this:
When I began to think about the work you commanded
I guarded my spirit, did not expend it
On trifles that were not to the point....

What happened?
My own recollected thought
Encountered the hidden potential in the wood;
From this live encounter came the work
Which you ascribe to the spirits."
(The Way of Chuang Tzu, 110–11)

This wisdom reminds us to offer the energy of work with intentionality, focus, and the inner freedom for self and others.

Work without meaning or recollection leads to boredom, depression, loneliness, and burnout. No wonder so many people can't wait for the weekends! As author Sam Keen astutely points out, upward mobility has usurped the ascent to discover the heights and depths of the human psyche (41–67). To earn a just salary means to earn a salary that is commensurate with the value of one's employment for the good of society and the environment. When this value is subjugated to the primary value of one's own infinite desires, then we are dealing with greed with its many different disguises and names. In many parts of our society, greed has been turned into a virtue, with no end in sight. How much is enough? Rather than seeing how much we can earn, would it not be better for society, our relationships, and the environment, to see how well we can live on what we earn? Of course, most of us must work to earn a living—that is not the question, the issue is about emphasis. Today many people work for the love of, or obsession with, money itself, as if it were a god, not for the sake of the work itself or for creative expression, as evidenced in the tremendous decline in volunteerism in America. This egocentric attitude of willfulness is contrary to the virtue of willingness to serve the greater good of society. This in turn creates a greater disparity between the extremely wealthy and the desperately poor.

Many people find their identity or self-esteem in what they do, rather than who they are. Whether we like it or not, work, paid or unpaid, is a necessary component of a fully functioning and satisfying adult life. This is one of the reasons unemployment and underemployment are such pernicious social illnesses. However, work now seems to carry many of the promises once proffered by religion. As author Warren Farrell points out, this new civil religion of prosperity carries with it the following underlying themes:

- Work status is the source of all blessings and happiness.
- Prosperity is a sign of progression to the Reign of God.
- Full employment is a sign of grace.
- Unemployment or underemployment is a sign of laziness, thus possibly sinful.
- Industriousness is characteristic of God's chosen people. (3–17)

A spirituality of work (activity) must be balanced by a spirituality of Sabbath rest or leisure (contemplation). I like the words of publisher and writer Gregory Pierce: "The spirituality of work is a disciplined attempt to align ourselves and our environment with God and to incarnate God's spirit in the world through all the effort (paid and unpaid) we exert to make the world a better place, a little closer to the way God would have things" (19).

Pierce offers some practical steps that you might consider to assist you in this "disciplined attempt":

- Place a small sacred object in your workplace to remind you of the meaning of your work.
- Turn a secular object into a sacred object by giving it a different symbolic meaning (e.g., the phone as symbol of human connection).
- Make a list of the blessings that your job brings you.
- Affirm a fellow employee.
- Do something unexpected and thoughtful for a competitor.
- Practice a random act of kindness for the newest employee or one who is hurting.
- Make a daily examination of conscience on how you treated others.
- Eat lunch with different people at various times.
- Join or organize a small faith-sharing group.
- Pray for the sick and suffering in your organization.
- Practice letting go of grudges.
- Make short acts of prayer throughout the day.
- Bring some beauty into the workplace (e.g., pictures, flowers).
- Participate in community-building activities.
- Avoid office gossip or tearing down others.
- Practice virtues of compassion, respect, honesty, loyalty, and listening.
- When stressed, take a few slow deep breaths or repeat a sacred word.

- Participate in a professional development course or seminar at least once a year.
- Exercise at least three or four times a week as a means of honoring your body and its limitations.
- Take a "mental health" day once every few months.
- Read a good book once a month (19).

A job pays the bills; a vocation is what we have been created for. Ideally, these two aspects of our lives would flow together in our career opportunities. When that does not happen, then it is imperative that we seek fulfillment through volunteer work, or by nurturing the reflective side of our work. The quality and attitude that we bring to our job also can augment our sense of job satisfaction. We need to create an environment of gratitude around us, thanking others for their service or good work. We should find something we love and do it, or do something new each day, especially if we have a boring job. Sharing unpleasant tasks is also a good way to pass the time. How do you create an enjoyable work environment? Currently, when harassment, bullying, discrimination, and favoritism seem to be commonplace in many workplaces, what better antidote is there than for you to create a more positive setting than the continuing practice of the good, the true, and the beautiful?

QUESTIONS

Do you enjoy your work or your career? Why or why not?

What is your vocation? What brings you joy?

What are some practical ways that you incorporate your faith into your workplace or daily work schedule?

How do you balance work and leisure in your life?

PRAYER FORMS

Praying with icons or symbols: Focusing on a particular sacred symbol as a touchstone for your intention.

Short, silent prayers of gratitude through the day: Giving thanks for the precious moments of the day or one's life.

Intercessions: Praying for a particular intention or person.

SPIRITUAL PRACTICES

Join a work party: Plan a work project with family or friends (for example, cleaning out the garage, painting a room, or small remodeling project).

Do volunteer work: Join a local civic group or church organization that shares your values. Participate in a single project or ongoing networking of support.

Donate to a charity that invests in job training for the underprivileged: Locally or globally (for example, Catholic Relief Services, Youth4Jobs, Asha Deep Foundation).

Read a good self-help book: For example, David Richo, PhD., *How to Be an Adult: A Handbook for Psychological and Spiritual Integration* (New York/Mahwah, NJ: Paulist Press, 1991).

FURTHER READING

Donnelly, Doris. *Spiritual Fitness: Everyday Exercises for Body and Soul*. San Francisco: Harper & Row, 1993.

Oliva, Max. *Beatitudes for the Workplace*. Mystic, CT: Twenty-Third Publications, 2009.

Palmer, Parker. *The Active Life: A Spirituality of Work, Creativity and Caring*. San Francisco: Harper & Row, 1990.

Pierce, Gregory. *Spirituality at Work: 10 Ways to Balance Your Life on-the-Job*. Chicago: Loyola Press, 2001.

17

Soulful Living
Get Your Act Together!

(Depression/Malaise)

DEPRESSION IS THE NUMBER-ONE mental illness in North America. At last count, it appears that the general category of depression accounts for approximately 75 percent of the reported cases of mental illness. While there are different causes, classes, and categories of depression, this statistic should make us all pause and reflect on the significance of this situation. What does this say about our culture in the twenty-first century from the point of view of sociology, psychology, and spirituality? When we look at the body of reading material currently being offered to the general public on this topic, the striking factor is the increased number of books written on human happiness and suffering. Perhaps one way to look at this area of cultural concern is to notice the disconnect between the external and the internal lives of many people. Many of us have compartmentalized lives, with no real grounding in our best and truest self, our soul. This is the purpose of life—to become human/whole/happy by connecting with all aspects of our being.

In John 1:38, we encounter Jesus' telling question to two men, "What are you looking for?" We must all answer this question in one way or another. What do you really want from life? What nourishes your inner life? What gives you joy or makes you truly happy? To participate in the daily crafting of a joy-filled life is the necessary work of every human being. Thomas Aquinas puts it this way, "To be happy is perhaps the most moral thing that one could do." Letting go of unreal expectations of ourselves and our reality is a good place to start. This is one way to address the irritating malaise in our lives.

Many of us are encouraged by reading the biographies of great explorers of yesteryear or contemporary researchers of the ocean depths or outer space. Perhaps no more than at any other time in human history, we need great explorers of inner space—people willing to dive into the depths of the human soul to discover God's immanent presence.

Searching for God in all things is the work of the soul explorer, the wise person, the lover. The author of the Book of Ecclesiastes declares, "There is a time for everything." This is ancient wisdom, reminding us that our lives are multidimensional. No one part is to dominate the others unduly. Every part has its place and its particular importance. If sexuality is the vibrancy of life, soulful living is the container or greenhouse for that vibrancy, where it can grow and come to fullness.

One of the most common biblical images used to describe the reign of God is the wedding banquet where everyone is welcome. This is a wonderful image to bring to our lives—to accept and welcome all aspects of our being, recognizing that the inner world is a reflection of the outer world, and vice versa. Attending to the yearnings, regrets, hopes, and dreams of our lives is a soulful and salvific task. Rather than sit back and simply let things unfold, we need to enter into dialogue with our pain, and our happiness, in order to discover our inner source and thus become free. This inner liberation will then have a noticeable effect on our outer reality.

Learning to live with paradox and the big questions of life is a sign of maturity. In the Indian culture, people are taught to treat the unexpected as a guest. Look for the gift. Dialogue with the unexpected and you will be less likely to feel depressed or victimized by reality. A good number of things are, in fact, out of your control. Ask yourself, "Now that this has happened, how do I want to live the rest of my life?" We cannot change the past, but we can change the way we live the present. Embracing the questions of life opens the inner chambers of the soul in order that we might be awakened to the richness of our full identity.

Our attitudinal approach to reality and to life means everything. Mark Twain recommends, "Let us endeavor so to live that when we come to die even the undertaker will be sorry." Not a bad idea! One way to put this into practice is to reverence the natural rhythm of reality. There is a time for everything in our day, our life, if we discipline ourselves. When we punctuate our day with breaks, rest periods, or energy shifts, we are likely to find life becoming richer, more mindful. The narrative of our day has a built-in fullness that only needs the space to reveal its essential beauty. In my busy life, I have discovered the very simple but pleasant gift of a tea break. Each morning and afternoon, I take an herbal tea break as a means of slowing myself down, and shifting my energy. Sometimes I even use this time as a "reward" for completing some small task. There is a time to work and a time for leisure. Honoring this rhythm is the humanizing aspect to our existence—the space between the musical notes of our daily activities.

Psychoanalyst Thomas Moore has written extensively on honoring the soul in our daily lives. His eclectic approach presents a holistic lens through which we might observe our lives in order to make some adjustments. Drawing on our own interior knowledge and strengths liberates us from the shackles of others' expectations. This approach can ground us in living from our inner authenticity—our true self. Connecting with our own imagination and dreams is a good starting point. Here are some areas you might want to reflect upon as a means of expressing and caring for your own soul:

- Family, friends, warm relationships
- Access to good literature, art, music, poetry
- Leisure, fun
- Nature and all its beauty
- Variety of good food and wine
- Meaningful employment
- Appreciation of history
- Understanding of culture
- Diversity in local community
- Sense of belonging to a community

- Travel and recreation
- Aesthetically pleasing house and environment
- Access to a garden
- Vibrant prayer life
- Meaningful spiritual practices
- Attention to good health: physical, emotional, intellectual, and spiritual
- Connection with larger world/cosmos
- Aesthetics of color and scent
- Appropriate attention to financial security to live comfortably within one's means
- Incorporation of ritual, dream tending, active imagination, symbolic expression, and stories
- Greater openness to passion and awe
- A choice to live in the moment
- A sense of deep gratitude (*The Soul's Religion*)

Thanks to some recent developments in science, we are beginning to see the convergence of different fields of study that have begun to impact the study of theology. What scientists are now discovering in the links between the human sciences (anthropology, sociology, psychology) and the natural sciences (quantum physics, cosmology, microbiology) is having a direct impact on the health and well-being of humans. Recent research in the field of brain studies, for example, has affirmed that inner space and outer space are connected. This has opened up wonderful creative possibilities for healing trauma. My friend Pat has had a lifelong struggle with generalized depression. It has been exacerbated by unhealthy family dynamics and struggles. One of the things I admire about Pat is that she is a fighter—defending her interior life. As a regular means of proclaiming her inner beauty and keeping her sanity, she gardens and draws. Her artwork is spectacular! Pat has especially gravitated to drawing animals and beautiful doorways. Here we have a wonderful example of someone who's living the symbolic life—she is expressing her instinctual nature and feelings through a loving depiction of animals, and the thresholds that they bring her to and through—pain, self-doubt, and the desire to be loved. In the end, Pat realizes she is the only one who can reclaim herself. Her determination will save her life.

QUESTIONS

How do you live so that when you come to die there will be no regrets?

How can you honor all aspects of your being?

What dreams and hopes do you have for yourself?

PRAYER FORMS

Prayer of gratitude: A simple "thank you" for what is, or for a particular blessing.

Growing appreciation of God's presence in everyday reality: Acknowledging the Creator's abiding presence in all aspects of reality.

Audio divina (divine music): Choosing and listening to a particular piece of music that uplifts your spirit.

SPIRITUAL PRACTICES

Writing poetry: Composing a creative written expression of your interior perceptions or experiences.

Visiting museums and art galleries: Seeing and learning about the best and worst of humankind's various expressions.

Gardening: Co-creating with the Creator.

Massage therapy: Honoring your body with a healing touch, especially good for traumatized persons.

Focus on the good, the true, and the beautiful: Seek out the best of being human and celebrate it.

Mini-sabbaticals: Make time for relaxation, leisure, and rest daily, weekly, monthly, and annually.

FURTHER READING

Benner, David G. *Soulful Spirituality: Becoming Fully Alive and Deeply Human.* Grand Rapids, MI: Brazos Press, 2011.

Moore, Thomas. *Care of the Soul: A Guide for Cultivating Depth and Sacredness in Everyday Life.* New York: HarperCollins, 1992.

Muller, Wayne. *Sabbath: Finding Rest, Renewal, and Delight in Our Busy Lives.* New York: Bantam Books, 1999.

Nouwen, Henri J. M. *Life of the Beloved: Spiritual Living in a Secular World.* New York: Crossroad, 1992.

Wright, Wendy. *Sacred Dwelling: A Spirituality of Family Life.* Leavenworth, KS: Forest of Peace Publishing, 1994.

18

Signs of Holiness
How Am I Doing?

(Reality vs. Appearance)

SOME ECCLESIAL GROUPS have hijacked the word *holiness* and have made it synonymous with and limited to piety or the following of a purity code. Rather, *holiness*, a word sharing the same root as *wholeness*, encompasses the whole of the Christian economy as it was lived out in Christ Jesus. Holiness is contextualized in time and place through the unique experience and life story of the individual. Our two-thousand-year-old Christian tradition demonstrates clearly that one size does not fit all. What, then, is the holiness that we are called to?

- Holiness is not about goodness. We are already good by virtue of our creation. God loves us because God is good, not because we are good. Holiness is about desiring God, the source of all goodness, above all.
- Holiness is not about increased devotion or prayer. These religious elements are possible ways to holiness but they are not signs of holiness. They can point us in the direction of God but they can also become a source of self-idolatry. Rather, holiness involves growth in inner freedom, balanced with a respect for outer authority.

- Holiness is not about right doctrine, right thinking, or even right worship. Holiness is about right practice—doing good for others. It is living the heroic life of virtue at all times.
- Holiness is not about separation from evil, but rather an absorption and transformation of evil. Holiness moves us from the myth of retaliatory violence to the divine plan of redemptive forgiveness. This is the authentic suffering of one who is growing in holiness.
- Holiness is not about worshipping creation or beauty. Rather, holiness is the act of embracing the whole of life in all its forms and expressions. Sin closes us down while grace opens us up to the wide horizons of God's presence and activity.
- Holiness is not about being with the right people. Holiness is about right relationship with all people.
- Holiness is not so much what you do but how you respond to what is done to you.
- Holiness is not about being nice or appearing spiritual. Holiness is the reality of living an authentic life, living beyond the expected norm of a culture or group. For this reason, a healthy spirituality is necessarily countercultural.
- Holiness is a growth process that takes time. There is no quick road to holiness; no special tricks, only the work of faithfulness to the inner life.

Many people think that by simply going to church, they will grow in holiness. This is as shortsighted and silly as sitting in a garage thinking that you will become a car one day. Holiness doesn't happen to you; it flows from your inner work and cooperation with God's grace. It is a process of interiorization. We participate in a church community to assist us in growing in authenticity by facing the reality of our lives, not by appearing holy.

Every culture and religion has chosen heroes and heroines who encapsulate the ideals of an authentic humanity. The stories of these men and women fire our imaginations and our own yearnings to be whole and holy. So how can you tell that you or others are growing in holiness (wholeness)? Here are ten signs or fruits of authentic inner work, the manifestation of a vibrant spirituality:

1. **Equanimity and serenity.** How do you respond to what is done to you? How do you respond to someone who ridicules you, abuses you, disrespects you, or hurts you? How do you react to a person who disagrees with you or your position? Think of the lack of civil discourse in political and religious circles today. What do you do when you are rejected or abandoned? In the end, equanimity and serenity are ultimately the proper response.

   Several years ago, Richard Rohr gave a presentation at a large conference in southern California. At the end of the talk there was an opportunity for individuals to ask questions or make comments. The first young man got up to the microphone and spent five minutes belittling Richard and his talk. At the conclusion of his insulting comments, Richard responded kindly by thanking him and telling him he would give his comments some thought. Next to the microphone was another young man who spent his time gushing with praise for Richard and his ideas. Richard responded with equal kindness and gratitude. Neither comment affected his serene demeanor because he knows who he is—a beloved son of God.

2. **Deep-seated gratitude.** Authentic gratitude does not necessarily depend upon external circumstances. Gratitude is another name for a deep appreciation for life in all its different manifestations (friendships, food, drink, music, art, beauty, sexuality, creation). A love of embodied celebration pervades the holy person's life. Appreciating life and living it to the full is the highest form of praise of the Creator. This is manifested in authentic kindness through active works of caregiving. Gratitude is the antidote to greed in all its many forms of expression.

   Legendary social justice advocate and activist Dorothy Day said that what really set her out on her journey of seeking God was the birth of her daughter. She said, "For such great beauty I must find someone to thank."

3. **Compassionate response to suffering that is translated into action.** The human condition includes suffering in all its many forms (personal, familial, communal, national, cosmic). Choosing not to pass judgment on the suffering of another is a good starting point in caring for others. Demonizing the other (stranger, immigrant, foreigner, liberal, conservative) is only a way of escaping our common responsibility to care for others. How I respond to the suffering at my own doorstep is the real moral test. Sympathy is simply feeling sorry for the person or situation; compassion moves us to an active response.

On one of his first journeys to India, Jungian psychoanalyst Robert Johnson was accosted by a group of impoverished children beseeching him for some small gift. In his desire to do good, Robert reached into his pocket and gave coins to the children. After the children left, his guide rebuked him for his actions. "You Americans are all the same," said the guide. "You always want to throw money at a situation hoping to better it, when in reality it is about feeling better about yourself in the face of suffering." Robert was stunned by the rebuke but it made him think about how he could honestly help his beloved India. He knew he couldn't help everyone. Finally, he hit upon the idea of helping to support one family in a village. This allowed the family to eventually purchase fishing supplies to raise their income and that of the village.

4. **Praying in all situations.** Making a commitment to prayer and growing intimacy with God is an expression of faith and respect for the inner life, a dedication to honoring the sacredness of life. This kind of commitment seeks to find God in all things, situations, and persons, especially the small and vulnerable, the lost and forsaken. Prayer centers us, grounds us, and reminds us of who we are. Without real prayer, there will be a disjunctive split within you. The transfiguration is a symbol of what prayer can do to a person. All of Jesus is permeated with the light of Divine Love (dazzling clothes) and everything (external world) is transformed.

The psalms are filled with every imaginable human emotion, demonstrating that we can and ought to pray within and through all of life's different phases. Praying only when we need something or when we are feeling happy is self-centered; praying at all times is building a relationship with the Divine.

5. **Peaceful response to violence or oppression.** Our enemies are meant to wake us up to our own unredeemed dark side. I remember being deeply moved by a line from the movie *Gandhi*—a quote that may or may not have been attributable to the man himself, but seems to carry profound wisdom: "I want to spend the rest of my life only with those who disagree with me, for it is they who have much to teach me." Choosing a bias toward forgiveness, reconciliation, and conflict resolution demands a stance of humility toward reality. The violence without activates the violence within, unless there is a conscious choice and discipline to move in the path of forgiveness and peace.

   What a lesson we can all learn from the Amish community in Nickel Mines, Pennsylvania. On October 2, 2006, Charles Roberts IV, entered the one-room elementary school and shot ten girls, aged six to thirteen, killing five of them and then in turn, ending his own life. The families of the community responded with such gracious forgiveness that it generated a national discussion about the place of forgiveness and reconciliation in the face of random acts of violence.

6. **Active response to injustice.** True worship flows into active works of justice for others. We all desire personal mercy and personal justice but the holy person seeks mercy and justice for all. All lives are important, equal in the sight of God. Color of skin, socioeconomic status, religious affiliation, cultural background, gender, sexual orientation, abilities, or educational training do not separate us in God's perspective or realm. We are all God's family. Courageously responding to injustice is an indication of hope and a work of authentic healing.

Frances, a skilled and educated woman, had a desire to express her faith in action and so felt drawn to serve the poor. But how? As she thought and reflected, she decided to help at St. Mary's soup kitchen every week. She was surprised to discover that her weekly encounter began to affect other areas of her life as well. Frances soon learned that she received more from the poor and homeless than she shared with them.

7. **Relationships that are holistic and respectful.** We become like the god(s) we worship. Belief in a trinitarian God teaches us that God is mutual, equal, and reciprocal in the divine communion. We have been created in relationship for relationship. This is meant to translate practically and ideally into spending our lives learning how to receive love and then to share love with others. This is manifested in a compassionate approach to all human vicissitudes. This attitude offers a broad anthropological view of the mystery of what it means to be human, embracing the many differences of humanity, blessing individuals in the process.

I once heard this story recounted by psychoanalyst Robert Johnson: Many years ago in a small village in Japan, there was a married couple who raised their daughter in the traditional manner. When it was time, the father arranged for their daughter's marriage to an only son who lived with his elderly father. After the marriage ceremony, at their first meal at home, the new wife noticed that her father-in-law sat apart from her husband and herself. He was given a wooden bowl to eat his rice from while they had porcelain bowls. Her father had warned her not to question her husband in anything. So she decided to wait and question her father-in-law. After the meal, he informed her of the painful division between himself and his son over a past grievance. She encouraged him to break his wooden bowl. Despite his protestations, he did as he was told. The next meal as she dutifully served rice to her husband, she feigned surprise that her father-in-law had broken his dish. Her husband was incensed. He stood up and loudly insulted his father, "You should not have done that, old man. For now you will eat rice out of your hands." The wife graciously bowed to her husband and said, "You are right dear husband. He should not have done such a thing, for I was saving that bowl for you so that your children could serve you rice in it."

8. **Transparency.** Facing the truth about oneself and about reality is perhaps the most challenging aspect of the maturing process of becoming fully human. Truth, whether discovered or revealed, is our friend in the work of seeing ourselves as God sees us. Letting go of our undue attachments and our false self is the necessary work of waking up to our own divinized nature. This is authentic humility.

This is the real work of twelve-step programs—to help people grow in honesty and transparency. I have seen and experienced this patient, liberating work in several acquaintances who have submitted to this process.

9. **Integrity.** The integration of the whole person is the work of salvation, the work of God. We cannot be compartmentalized for very long without doing serious damage to our lives. The very nature of our bodies teaches us this truth. Compartmentalization or disintegration is a way of escaping the pain of being human. Integrating the physical, emotional, intellectual, spiritual, and instinctual aspects of our humanity is the artistic and necessary work of the mature human being. This leads to inner cohesion and emotional congruence. Wisdom is the daily application of this process.

At her retirement party, Joan was surprised to hear the accolades about her. Many of her colleagues and managers spoke of feeling an aura about her or a sense of calmness in her presence. Others explained the experience of her work with them as healing and connecting. In a word, they were describing Joan's integrity as a person, as a believer.

10. **All-embracing world view.** Seeing as God sees is the invitation of the Creator. This vision is not just for the future reign of God. It is for the here and now. All is one. Somehow, it all fits together. Anchorite Julian of Norwich said it beautifully: "All shall be well,

and all shall be well, and all manner of things shall be well." This seamless culture of life has been called a consistent life ethic. Honoring the work of integration of the whole means that we fully participate as co-creators in respecting all aspects of creation. This is then telescoped into the whole cosmos. Starting with the particular, we then move outward to the universal or cosmic experience of reality. This work is manifested in joy.

Many years ago, I made a guided vision quest that incorporated this Lakota wilderness tradition with the Christian faith experience. This very transformative experience culminated in a sweat lodge, a purification ritual. After coming out of the intense sweat, I was escorted to the lake where I floated in the cool waters for a time, looking up at the starry midnight sky. All at once, I saw and understood how it all fit together—light and dark, heaven and earth, here and there. It made sense to me; everything belongs together! Somehow, God is both within and yet beyond it all.

Over the long haul, if you do not notice yourself growing in these areas of life and relationship, then perhaps you might consider adjusting or changing the forms of prayer or elements of your spiritual practices. Your spirituality nourishes and sustains both your inner and your outer life. The fruit that it bears will be in accordance with what you provide. One of the purposes of prayer, indeed, is to grow in virtue. We do this work in order to be transformed into the glory of God (Rom 12:2)—to become the persons God intended us to be—truly, uniquely human—for our own good and the good of others!

QUESTIONS

Who are your models of holiness? Are they exclusively canonized saints or do they include people close at hand?

Do you recognize any holiness in yourself?

Which areas might be open for more growth?

PRAYER FORMS

Choose a prayer form relating to the particular category (from the previous chapters) that stretches you and leads you into new territory and will support you in your desired area of growth: daily, weekly, and monthly.

Seek out mentors to assist you on your journey.

FURTHER READING

Keating, Charles J. *Who We Are is How We Pray: Matching Personality and Spirituality.* Mystic, CT: Twenty-Third Publications, 1987.

Moore, Thomas. *The Soul's Religion: Cultivating a Profoundly Spiritual Way of Life.* New York: HarperCollins, 2002.

Nicholl, Donald. *Holiness.* New York: Seabury Press, 1981.

Sinetar, Marsha. *Ordinary People as Monks and Mystics: Lifestyles for Spiritual Wholeness.* New York/Mahwah, NJ: Paulist Press, 1986.

Tuoti, Frank X. *Why Not Be a Mystic?* New York: Crossroad, 1995.

Setting Out for the Future
Where Do We Go from Here?

WHEN I WAS A BOY, my father used to play catch with me, helping me to improve my baseball technique. Throwing the ball back and forth over and over again provided the opportunity for many a conversation. For me this is a wonderful image of God. God desires to work with me, to help me improve, to grow in happiness. This desire is manifested in God's ever-present, self-communicating love. God has started the conversation. It is up to me to continue it—to throw the ball back to God. This is called prayer. The back-and-forth conversation sustains the relationship and strengthens me in the process.

Our image of God will affect everything we do and everything we believe about ourselves.

How do you image God? Do you see God as a Divine Mother or Father, or perhaps as an Ocean of Love, Mountain of Strength, or Judge? I hope that as you continue to "play catch with God" in prayer, your image of God and yourself will evolve into a growing appreciation of your partnership with God. God always and everywhere is present to you on your journey of life.

God desires that you become the heart and hands of God on earth, letting love, healing, compassion, blessing, and forgiveness flow through you and around you (Morwood). Be expansive and big-hearted, like the cosmos. Create relationships that are vibrant and mutually satisfying, let go of attachments to past hurts. Live in the moment and delight in the gift of life.

At one level, it is all so simple: receive life, experience life, and share life. This is our task as human beings, whether at home or at work. Focusing on the good, the true, and the beautiful in our conversations, our responsibilities, and our relationships helps us to live from our interior centeredness. It reminds us to live from our essence, to be authentic.

The Gospel of Luke contains several stories of wholeness. Each parable contains the following elements:

- Finding what's lost
- Embracing what's rejected
- A passion for inclusion
- When inclusion (wholeness) takes place, we celebrate

This is the ongoing work of the spiritual life—to seek out that which is lost, alienated, or rejected, whether in ourselves or others, to embrace it and include it at the "banquet table" of our attention (Shea). This is courageous work, a transforming lifelong task.

I leave you with a final story. A priest friend of mine, Fr. Rick, shared with me his own version of playing catch with God. When the abuse scandal in the Catholic Church broke wide open, Fr. Rick was, like all of us, devastated. When he brought this situation and his feelings to prayer, he felt prompted to focus on an image of a banquet table or large altar. In his imagination, Fr. Rick saw all the different aspects of his own person gathered around the table: there was the great friend, the good priest, the counselor, the wise teacher, the helpful professional. He felt quite affirmed in his own goodness. As he continued to pray with this image over time, he was surprised when other manifestations of his personhood began to present themselves for attention: the gossip, the petty cleric, the liar, and even to his great dismay, the officious judge. As Fr. Rick allowed this image and conversation to work on him, he began to notice some gradual changes in his life. He found himself becoming less impatient and judgmental, and more compassionate to the suffering and pain of others. In a word, this man experienced transformation. Transformation is God's dream for *all* of us.

Ready to play catch?

Works Cited

Bausch, William. *A World of Stories for Preachers and Teachers*. Mystic, CT: Twenty-Third Publications, 1998.

Bourgeault, Cynthia. *The Wisdom Way of Knowing: Reclaiming Ancient Tradition to Awaken the Heart*. San Francisco: Jossey-Bass, 2003.

Brueggemann, Walter. *The Creative Word: Canon as Model for Biblical Education*. Philadelphia: Fortress Press, 1982.

Campbell, Joseph. *Thou Art That: Transforming Religious Metaphors*. Novato, CA: New World Library, 2001.

Campbell, Joseph, and Bill Moyers. *The Power of Myth*. New York: Knopf Doubleday Publishing Group, 2011.

Chittister, Joan, OSB. "Labor Day: A Spirituality of Work." *Huffington Post*. Sept. 6, 2010. www.huffingtonpost.com.

————. *Welcome to Wisdom of the World and Its Meaning for You: Universal Spiritual Insights Distilled from Five Religious Traditions*. Grand Rapids, MI: Eerdmans, 2007.

de Waal, Esther. *Seeking God: The Way of St. Benedict*. Collegeville, MN: The Liturgical Press, 2001.

Farrell, Warren. *Why Men Earn More*. New York: AMACOM, 2005.

Jäger, Willigis. *Search for the Meaning of Life: Essays and Reflections on the Mystical Experience*. Liguori, MO: Liguori/Triumph, 1989.

Keen, Sam. *Fire in the Belly: On Being a Man*. New York: Bantam Books, 1991.

May, Gerald G. *Will and Spirit: A Contemplative Psychology*. San Francisco: HarperOne, 1982.

Merton, Thomas. *Conjectures of a Guilty Bystander.* New York: Doubleday, 1965.

————. *New Seeds of Contemplation.* London: Burns & Oates, 2002.

————. *The Way of Chuang Tzu.* New York: New Directions, 1965.

Moore, Thomas. *The Soul's Religion: Cultivating a Profoundly Spiritual Way of Life.* New York: Perennial/HarperCollins, 2002.

Morwood, Michael. *Faith, Hope, and a Bird Named George.* New London, CT: Twenty-Third Publications, 2011.

Oliver, Mary. *Evidence: Poems.* Boston: Beacon Press, 2009.

Pierce, Gregory. *Spirituality of Work: 10 Ways to Balance Your Life on the Job.* Chicago: Loyola Press, 2001.

Plaskow, Judith. *Standing Again at Sinai: Judaism from a Feminist Perspective.* San Francisco: HarperOne, 1991.

Rohr, Richard. *Everything Belongs: The Gift of Contemplative Prayer.* New York: Crossroad, 2003.

————. *Falling Upward: A Spirituality for the Two Halves of Life.* San Francisco: Jossey-Bass, 2011.

————. "Pure Passion: The Holiness of Human Sexuality." *Sojourners* (Oct.–Nov. 1982): 30–32.

Rolheiser, Ronald. *The Holy Longing: The Search for a Christian Spirituality.* New York: Doubleday, 1999.

Ruffing, Janet, RSM. "Resisting the Demon of Busyness." *Spiritual Life* (Fall 2009): 147–59.

Shea, John. *Gospel Food for Hungry Christians: Luke: Image and Reflections from the Gospel.* CD Series. Skokie, IL: ACTA, 2008.

Whyte, David. "Revelation Must Be Terrible." In *Fire in the Earth.* Langley, WA: Many Rivers Press, 1992.